# DILEMMAS
OF
# LEADERSHIP

George B. Vaughan
and Associates

# DILEMMAS
## —— OF ——
# LEADERSHIP

Decision Making
and Ethics in
the Community
College

Foreword by Clark Kerr

Jossey-Bass Publishers
San Francisco

For sales outside the United States contact Maxwell Macmillan International Publishing Group, 866 Third Avenue, New York, New York 10022

Manufactured in the United States of America

The paper used in this book is acid-free and meets the State of California requirements for recycled paper (50 percent recycled waste, including 10 percent postconsumer waste), which are the strictest guidelines for recycled paper currently in use in the United States.

10% POST CONSUMER WASTE

**Library of Congress Cataloging-in-Publication Data**

Vaughan, George B.
    Dilemmas of leadership : decision making and ethics in the community college / George B. Vaughan and associates. — 1st ed.
      p.   cm.—(The Jossey-Bass higher and adult education series)
    Includes bibliographical references and index.
    ISBN 1-55542-468-6 (alk. paper)
    1. Community colleges—United States—Administration—Moral and ethical aspects.  2. Community college presidents—United States—Professional ethics.  3. Leadership—Moral and ethical aspects.
    I. Title.   II. Series.
LB2341.V343    1992
378'.052'0973—dc20                          92-8187
                                            CIP

FIRST EDITION
*HB Printing*    10 9 8 7 6 5 4 3 2 1               *Code 9263*

The Jossey-Bass
Higher and Adult Education Series

Consulting Editor
Community Colleges

Arthur M. Cohen
University of California, Los Angeles

# Contents

ix

# Foreword

Ethical conduct in the United States is under greater scrutiny now than perhaps at any other time since the days of the Puritans in New England. There are good reasons for this, including reasons that pertain to colleges and universities. Most of the literature covering ethics in higher education consists, however, of attacks by outsiders that have elements of truth but go far beyond what the facts warrant, and of half-hearted defenses by insiders against specific charges. This book is a great exception. It is neither excessively aggressive nor defensive. On the contrary, I find it balanced in its approach and down-to-earth in the suggested remedies. This is what one would expect under the guidance of George Vaughan as editor; he is one of the best-informed people in the nation about community colleges.

The authors confine their discussion to community colleges, but it could be extended to all of higher education. This is not to suggest that all institutions face identical problems; for example, some large universities face greater temptations in the handling of big-time athletics and in relations with the corporate world than do community colleges. But most of the problems discussed here are duplicated everywhere, and the general guidelines for ethical conduct are the same everywhere.

One issue that applies specifically to community colleges, however, is whether they have an overall ethical role in our society. It has been charged that they are engaged in a great conspiracy to sabotage equality of opportunity and to perpetuate the class structure of a capitalist society. That issue is only briefly discussed here, but I agree with the answer that Arthur Cohen gives in Chapter Two: "any educational structure that opens its doors to all, grants absolution for previous academic sins, and assists people in rising above their station is righteous."

The book's contributors explore primarily specific problem areas, not this grand issue of ethical conduct. Joseph Hankin lists in Chapter Five more than sixty ethical dilemmas, and I can think of more that might be added. In going through his list, I felt as though I were making my way through a minefield, fearing to take another step. I have thought of all those college presidents, to paraphrase Tennyson, with ethical dilemmas to the right of them, ethical dilemmas to the left of them, ethical dilemmas in the front of them, and who yet must ride on!

This volume is written mostly for and about community college presidents, although to some extent also for and about trustees. This gives me some pause. It seems to me to place too much responsibility on the presidents and trustees, and too little on faculty members and students. At least as many or more of the actual ethical lapses are the responsibility of faculty members and students as of presidents and trustees. I only wish that more of the discussion acknowledged the brutal reality that all members of the college community can be guilty of errors and should give greater attention to ethics in making choices.

There is an uncertainty in these chapters about whether it is enough to heighten sensitivity to ethical issues or whether it is better to have some general guidelines or whether it is necessary also to have specific codes (laws) to control actions. I come down on the side of general internal guidelines but fear that the current trend is toward more specific commandments, increasingly made by external authorities, including the courts.

These two hesitations aside, *Dilemmas of Leadership* is the best book I have seen come out of the several sectors of higher education, treating as it does the practical day-to-day aspects of ethical practices on campus. Gone are the days, if they ever existed, when presidents could survive and prosper as just "body counters" (as the crude caricature had it), intent on maximizing income with formulas for attendance rates, or as skillful handlers of any problems that might otherwise attract public notice. The tests of performance, including ethical leadership, are now more numerous and more meaningful. Community colleges, in particular, are on the social firing line of contending forces and views in our society and thus face more than their share of difficult ethical decisions. Consequently, their leaders need more than their proportionate share of guidance, and this volume is an excellent place to start.

*Berkeley, California*                                                        Clark Kerr
*June 1992*

Dedicated to
Mama (1893-1959) and Daddy (1890-1969),
who taught me right from wrong
and never
let me forget which was which

# Preface

Since the founding of Harvard in 1636, higher education has been a major force in the nation's struggle to establish and maintain high ethical standards in all aspects of society. Higher education assumed, or was assigned, the role of interpreting U.S. democracy to a nation that has constantly struggled to put into practice such value-laden (and at times sexually, racially, and culturally biased) concepts as freedom, equality, and justice for all. Much like the major religions, higher education has been responsible for establishing and interpreting ethical standards as well as for maintaining them.

Establishing, interpreting, and maintaining ethical standards are challenges educational leaders face every day. To ignore these challenges is to court humiliation at the least and disaster at the worst. Some breaches of accepted ethical conduct make the headlines: the president of a major West Coast research university is accused of failing to monitor the management of the institution in a way that would have placed financial transactions beyond reproach; he resigns his position. The chancellor of a midwestern community college is accused of hiding cost overruns from the governing board; he resigns his position. Claims about "cold fusion" are shared with the academic community and the world; the claims are false; the researchers lose credibility, as well as their research center. A Nobel laureate falsifies his research; he admits his guilt and retracts earlier statements. A president of a southern university is accused of soliciting sex; he resigns his position.

The dilemmas faced by leaders in higher education have an ethical dimension that, if not adhered to, can result in disaster for individuals, institutions, and the image of higher education. Higher education has been throughout its history, and continues to be, a focal point for the debate about what constitutes ethical behavior. At the center of the debate, often, is the president of the institution, although the ethical dimensions of decision making are by no means limited to the president's office.

## Background

The members of colleges and universities have been both victors and victims in many of the ethical dilemmas now facing the campus and society. The 1960s brought about many needed reforms on the nation's campuses. Students have every right to help define the learning process to a greater degree than had been allowed throughout much of our history. And no one would deny students and faculty members the right to free speech (although with the "politically correct" movement on many campuses, it seems as if the right to speak freely is once again a major issue). Many campuses, however, have been left with few ethical boundaries as a result of the "anything goes," "me first" attitudes that became a part of the culture of our campuses and our society beginning in the 1960s.

One can speculate with some justification that throughout this period, college and university presidents, deans, and board members retreated from including moral judgments in decisions that often begged for such judgments—partly because they did not understand their role or even what was happening on their own campuses. Or they backed off because they believed the students were right, because they were afraid of losing their jobs, or because they believed that the campus should simply reflect events within society rather than provide ethical leadership.

Today, higher education on occasion acknowledges its role in setting ethical standards. For example, the medical profession has found it necessary to remind its members and its students that their decisions have an ethical base; schools of law and business have issued the same admonition. The educational leaders of the professional schools, by once again making ethics an important part of the curriculum, are acknowledging the obligation and role of higher education in dealing with broad ethical issues within society. Why this new emphasis on ethics? Why should community college leaders be concerned with values and leadership to a degree and in a way that they have often not been in the past? These questions lead to more questions.

How can the leaders of a complex organization such as the community college make daily decisions that are morally correct for the organization and for individuals within it and that ultimately create a healthier society for all citizens, without creating a climate on campus saturated by the "rage of moral indignation" that too often distorts and eventually kills debates on ethics? How can community college leaders create and maintain a climate on campus that serves the community, including business and industry, without compromising the institution's commitment to ethical standards? Is it possible to focus on leadership and values in the community college, while recognizing that ethical dilemmas are often inherent in even the most mundane and routine decisions and actions of leaders?

For several reasons, community college leadership serves as an excellent arena for examining the ethical dilemmas of leadership in higher education. First, more than any other segment of higher education, community college members are in daily contact with individuals from practically all parts of society. The community college, then, provides a logical forum and focus for the examination of leadership and values and of the ethical dilemmas faced by leaders in higher education. Second, if the members of the community college, who are proud of its good citizenship and the pragmatism its leaders bring to solving community problems, are to help society understand and participate in the debate on ethical standards, they must embrace and promote those standards in all college operations. If the community college is to fill the role of teacher in a society that is perpetually trying to heal the wounds of Watergate, the Contras, drug dealers and addicts, oil spills, wars, and corruption at all levels of government, its leaders must espouse and practice values that reconcile rather than divide. Third, if the community college is to serve its community and the nation effectively, its leaders must understand the ethical dimensions of leadership and promote values and practices that reflect them.

To place the community college in perspective, we should first note that its growth has been phenomenal. At one time in the 1960s, community colleges were opening at the rate of one a week, which consumed the energy, creativity, and time of presidents and board members in the unending tasks of enrolling students, constructing buildings, hiring faculty and staff, and developing basic programs of study.

During that time, little thought was given to the potential ethical dilemmas inherent in open-access admissions policies and comprehensive curricula. Moreover, many community college students were older than traditional students (their average age on most campuses was over twenty-eight), and from a practical point of view, any trace of in loco parentis (with the ethical guidance inherent in it) remaining after the 1960s consequently disappeared. Also, because the community college was founded on the belief that it should meet the needs of the community in which it was located—without challenging the existing culture—the need to debate moral issues at community colleges was less than it had traditionally been in higher education.

Having successfully weathered the boom years of community college development, why should community college members be actively concerned with leadership and values? Community colleges are in a position (geographically and philosophically) to react to changes and challenges in society with greater immediacy than can traditional institutions of higher education, which continue to be concerned primarily with educating members of society who are either academically or socioeconomically above average. Many community college students, by contrast, come from groups in society (blue-collar workers and their children, minorities, older working adults, women with grown children, and others) who have been and continue to be ignored by the more traditional institutions of higher education. Community colleges thus have the potential to reach and directly influence people that other segments of higher education do not. These colleges occupy that middle ground where traditional higher education and the workplace meet. Indeed, community colleges have replaced the concept of the student as citizen with the concept of the citizen as student. The reversal provides them with a unique opportunity to promote ethical values in ways that have an immediate impact on the daily lives of the citizen-student, who does not have to wait four years to graduate before entering the workplace and assuming the full rights and responsibilities of citizenship: many community college students have had these rights and responsibilities for years.

Community college leaders need a forum and focus for their leadership that permits and encourages them to emphasize values. That is, presidents and other leaders need to legitimate the debate on the ethical dilemmas inherent in leadership by making the debate an integral part of college culture. Without the stimulation and potential practical solutions to ethical dilemmas provided by discussion such as that in this volume, however, too few community college leaders are likely to engage in introspection about the relationship between leadership and values. Community colleges, as an important part of higher education, have a right and a responsibility to engage in the debates on ethical issues that have long been a part of the academic scene in the United States.

Any discussion of ethics in relation to community college leadership at once draws one into the larger debate on the role of ethical leadership within society. The relationship of community college leaders and society as a whole is especially complex, since community colleges pride themselves on reflecting the needs and values of the community in which they are located, even when the community promotes practices, say, that run counter to environmental health (strip-mining or the use of tobacco, for example). Certainly, community college leaders must not, and indeed cannot, exist in a vacuum or be limited by the values of any single segment of society, single community, or single moment in time.

Although few community college leaders have the time or

inclination to debate the ethical merits of routine decisions, they nevertheless must understand that the culture of the institution reflects those decisions. With that in mind, leaders can and should be concerned with, and help to shape, the principles, beliefs, and rules of conduct that guide the daily actions of members of the college community.

As suggested earlier, the question community college leaders face is how to create and maintain a campus climate that serves the larger society by helping people base their decisions on a sense of what is right. The challenge in creating such a climate is to place ethical discussion in the context of day-to-day campus activities and to offer practical solutions to the ethical dilemmas, when possible.

The chapter authors examine ethical issues from the perspective of leaders, scholars, and practitioners who daily face dilemmas inherent in their work. The solutions offered, while necessarily cast in the broader context of campus activity and society, are for the most part practical.

### Scope of the Book

*Dilemmas of Leadership* provides answers to many of the questions just posed. To bring focus to the discussion, however, it has been necessary and desirable to place some limits on what the book attempts to accomplish. The discussion is limited largely to issues that can be directly influenced by actions of the governing board or the president. Practical solutions are offered, when possible, to the ethical dilemmas faced by board members and presidents. Still, although practical solutions are offered, certain aspects of this or any debate on values and leadership remain philosophical. The best practical solution available at a given moment may be to raise and debate the issue rather than to provide answers. Many important ethical issues confronting higher education are not included in this book because of the nature of the community college itself. Community colleges do not participate in big-time athletics and do not conduct controversial research, for example; therefore, those subjects are not treated in this volume.

## Overview of the Contents

*Dilemmas of Leadership* is divided into three parts. Part One consists of three chapters that provide the basis for the remainder of the book.

In Chapter One, I give an overview of some of the ethical dilemmas leaders face in providing leadership in education, in the institution, and in the community and society. I ask and answer the question of what presidents and board members can do to maintain ethical balance in achieving the institution's mission. I also explore the role that institutional culture plays in creating a campus climate that promotes ethical decision making.

In Chapter Two, Arthur Cohen asks and answers the question of how the ethical dimensions of community colleges are viewed. Cohen seeks to discern the institution's guiding ethos. An important part of the chapter discusses what data institutions collect and how they use (or fail to use) the data.

In Chapter Three, Daniel Moriarty places the responsibility for ethical practices directly on the back of the president, a heavy but unavoidable burden. Yet seen in the light of themes presented in both this chapter and the book as a whole, that responsibility can also present a rare and often unexplored opportunity for leadership. Moriarty illustrates this point by outlining some of the opportunities community college presidents have to provide ethical leadership.

In Part Two, the focus of the discussion is narrowed. Concrete examples and specific ethical problems and practices are discussed in the context of the community college environment.

Chapter Four, by Florence Brawer, discusses educational leadership and ethics. Brawer makes the point that just a few years ago, to question ethics in the instructional program or in the classroom, at whatever level, would have appeared ludicrous to some educators. She believes, however, that if the community college is to achieve its potential as a moral force in society, its faculty members must be actively concerned with ethical issues ranging from ethics in the curriculum to ethics in the use of the computer.

In Chapter Five, Joseph Hankin provides a novel way of looking at serious ethical issues facing community college leaders. He gives examples of ethical dilemmas in student services, curricula, instructional activities, governance and college-community relations, budget and finance, and that perennial preoccupation of every leader, personnel matters.

Karen Bowyer, in Chapter Six, moves the discussion into the often nebulous area where community college leaders come face-to-face with business leaders. The author uses the phrase *institutions on the edge* to describe the business-industry partnership that most community colleges enter into. She examines both the positive and the negative results of such relationships and offers advice on how to avoid the pitfalls.

In Chapter Seven, the final chapter in Part Two, Gary Davis focuses on the role of the governing board in setting the ethical tone for an institution. What hidden agendas, if any, do trustees bring to their positions? What can be done to alter questionable behavior by trustees and boards, should it occur? The author explores these and other questions and gives practical advice on how to deal with ethical issues faced by most governing boards.

Part Three serves as the capstone to the book. Building on the previous chapters, Chapters Eight and Nine conclude the discussion as it began, on a realistic yet optimistic note.

In Chapter Eight, Charles Neff evaluates the ethical commitments inherent in the presidential search process. Neff maintains that the development of ethical leaders begins with the college board and its procedures for recruitment and selection of presidents.

The final chapter is written by James Tatum, long-time trustee and community college leader. The author alludes briefly to points made in the previous chapters, bringing his own unique perspective to the discussion. He believes that there is a logical pathway to follow in making ethical decisions. Pulling no punches, he criticizes trustees and presidents for skirting ethical issues and taking the easy way out. The author draws examples from his own experiences as a trustee to illustrate the complexity of a decision-making process based on ethical considerations.

## Audience

People in leadership positions who can influence the current and future development of the community college are the primary audience for this book. Important among these leaders are community college trustees and presidents. Presidents can play a critical part in ensuring that the issues discussed in this book are included in the debate on campus regarding the role of the community college. Another important audience comprises faculty members, administrators, and support staff, who play such important roles in determining whether the climate on campus results in a culture that enhances decision making based on accepted ethical values. In addition to these people who are directly concerned with the value system of the community college, leaders in other institutions of higher education and scholars of higher education will find that the ethical dilemmas they face differ in degree but not in kind from most of the ones discussed here. This book has something to offer them, as well. And people in programs designed to educate leaders of community colleges and other institutions of higher education should find the issues discussed here extremely valuable as they seek to understand the complexities of U.S. higher education.

## Acknowledgments

As with writing I have done in the past or hope to do in the future, the individual who deserves much of the credit for any success I enjoy is Peggy A. Vaughan. An astute scholar and writer, she always works to ensure that my work comes up to her standards, which are high indeed. As always, Peggy has taken a hand in shaping the work on which I am fortunate enough to put my name.

While I was still at George Mason University, Brenda Noel was an inspiration, a confidante, and an outstanding secretary. She invested herself in this book and its authors. James Palmer, also a former colleague of mine at George Mason, read my chapter and offered suggestions that greatly strengthened it.

Since arriving at the University of Florida, I have had the good fortune to profit from the wise counsel of James Wattenbarger. He, perhaps more than anyone, understands the value of the community college and the need for its leaders to take ethical considerations into account.

To my colleagues and coauthors, thank you for your untiring work to bring about this book. Your patience with me has kept me going, your knowledge has inspired me, and your good common sense has made the endeavor worthwhile.

Finally, it is rare today to find an editor who is willing to offer advice on a project even before it takes shape and who sees the project through to fruition. In this regard, we have indeed been fortunate to have the good counsel of Gale W. Erlandson, senior editor of the Jossey-Bass Higher and Adult Education Series. Recognizing that any shortcomings lie with us, the authors, we gratefully acknowledge that *Dilemmas of Leadership* is much stronger because of Gale's interest in the project and the many hours she put into seeing that the book became the best we could make it.

*Gainesville, Florida*                                    George B. Vaughan
*June 1992*

# The Authors

*George B. Vaughan* is professor of higher educational leadership at the University of Florida. From 1988 to 1991, he was director of the Center for Community College Education at George Mason University. From 1977 to 1988, he served as president of Piedmont Virginia Community College. He was the founding president of Mountain Empire Community College and dean of instruction at two other community colleges.

Vaughan received his B.A. degree (1959) in economics from Emory and Henry College, his M.A. degree (1965) in history from Radford University, and his Ph.D. degree (1970) in higher education from Florida State University. He also completed two years of post-master's degree work in history at the University of Tennessee.

Vaughan serves on the board of directors of the American Association of Community and Junior Colleges (AACJC) and is former chair of the AACJC's Presidents Academy. He is a member of the editorial boards of the *Educational Record, Review of Higher Education,* and *Community College Review.*

Vaughan has published articles in numerous journals, including *Change Magazine; Community, Technical, and Junior Colleges Journal; Review of Higher Education; Community Services Catalyst; Community College Frontiers; Educational Record; National Forum; Trustee Quarterly;* and *Community College Review.* He has edited and contributed chapters to works in the Jossey-Bass New Directions for Community Colleges series, including *Questioning the Community College Role, Maintaining Institutional Integrity,* and *Enhancing Teaching and Administration Through Scholarship.* Among his books are *Issues for Community College Leaders in a New Era* (1983), *The Community College Presidency* (1986), *Leadership in Transition* (1989), and *Pathway to the Presidency* (1990).

In 1988, he was named one of the fifty most effective community college presidents in the nation. He has served as a consultant to colleges in several states.

*Karen A. Bowyer* is president of Dyersburg State Community College in Tennessee. For twelve years, she worked at Shelby State Community College, where she served as instructor of mathematics, department head, dean of instruction, and interim president. She is a member of the board of directors of the American Association of Community and Junior Colleges, the National Junior College Athletic Association, the Council on Adult and Experiential Learning, and the Tennessee Humanities Council. She holds a Ph.D. degree (1971) in mathematics from the University of Alabama.

*Florence B. Brawer* is research director of the Center for the Study of Community Colleges. She received her Ed.D. degree (1967) in educational psychology from the University of California, Los Angeles. She is the author of *New Perspectives on Personality Development in College Students* (1976), the coauthor of *The American Junior College* (1989), and the coeditor of volume three of *Developments in the Rorschach Technique* (1970).

*Arthur M. Cohen* has been a professor of higher education at the University of California, Los Angeles, since 1964. He received his Ph.D. degree (1964) in higher education from Florida State University. He is the director of the ERIC Clearinghouse for Junior Colleges and president of the Center for the Study of Community Colleges. His extensive writings include *Dateline '79: Heretical Concepts for the Community College* (1969) and *The American Junior College* (1989, with Florence B. Brawer).

*Gary W. Davis* is the executive director of the Illinois Community College Trustees Association. He has published articles on college governance, intellectual history, religion, and ethics. Davis taught humanities (1970–1981) at Northwest Missouri State University before accepting administrative posts in Michigan and Illinois. He holds a Ph.D. degree (1972) in religion and ethics from the University of Iowa.

*Joseph N. Hankin* is president of Westchester Community College in New York and adjunct professor in the Department of Higher and Adult Education at Teachers College, Columbia University. He earned his Ed.D. degree (1967) in administration of higher education, with a specialization in community colleges, from Teachers College. His community college research interests include community services, collective bargaining, affirmative action, and the community college mission.

*Daniel F. Moriarty* has been president of Portland Community College in Oregon since 1986. He received his Ed.D. degree (1974) from George Washington University. He has served as chair of the AACJC's Presidents Academy and is currently president of COMBASE.

*Charles B. Neff* is vice president for the Presidential Search Consultation Service of the Association of Governing Boards. He has assisted more than thirty higher education institutions in hiring presidents. He received his Ph.D. degree (1961) in international relations from Yale University. He has served as associate vice-chancellor for the State University of New York, as president of the Associated Colleges of the Midwest, and in several administrative capacities at the University of Wisconsin, River Falls.

*James B. Tatum,* trustee at Crowder College in Missouri for three decades, has served as a consultant, speaker, or facilitator at over 150 community colleges. He is the recipient of the M. Dale Ensign Outstanding Trustee Award from the Association of Community College Trustees, the Trustee Leadership Award from the American Association of Community and Junior Colleges, and the Distinguished Service Award from the Association of Governing Boards.

# DILEMMAS
## OF
# LEADERSHIP

**Part One**

# Leadership and Ethics in Today's Community Colleges

# Chapter One

# Leaders on a Tightrope: The Risks and Tensions of Community College Leadership

## George B. Vaughan

The focus of this book is on community college leadership and the ethical dilemmas inherent in this leadership. Ethical dilemmas are nothing new to community college leaders. They have always found themselves on that precarious edge where higher education interacts with the larger society. Corporate leaders have often asked community colleges to serve the needs of business and industry and thus to ignore the needs of others. Other special interest groups have demanded certain programs and courses. Politicians have asked that friends and relatives be employed or admitted to certain programs. Four-year institutions have attempted to dictate academic standards through transfer programs. Limited resources have required that certain groups be served and others ignored, often raising moral issues. And the tensions resulting from a system of funding based on the number of students enrolled have forced leaders to face constant ethical dilemmas.

In each of these situations, the leaders have had to make decisions that go well beyond good administrative practices. For example, the decision to place a large amount of institutional resources into the college transfer program while providing no funding for those students who require developmental education presents a potential ethical dilemma in an open-access community college. To point out that community college leaders have always faced ethical dilemmas helps place the debate in perspective. This realization can also help leaders deal with the dilemmas in today's environment.

What ethical dilemmas do community college leaders face today? The current environment is one in which dilemmas of the past remain. Politicians still want friends employed or admitted, business leaders still place their needs above the needs of others, and the funding nightmare will not go away.

In addition, the current environment places new pressures on leaders. Resources are more limited than in the past two decades. The pressures have increased to enroll students for funding purposes, regardless of the match between the student and the institution. The state of the economy has increased the pressure on politicians to find jobs for friends and relatives. And as four-year institutions place limits on the number of transfer students, community college leaders have to decide what promises can be kept regarding transfer programs.

Economic restraints, while not new, have new dimensions today. For example, political leaders in Florida are once again questioning whether community colleges should offer precollege courses, thereby jeopardizing the open-access comprehensive mission of the community college. Over the past decade, Virginia's community colleges have enrolled approximately 17,000 full-time-equivalent students with no increase in financial resources. The California State University System is reevaluating the admission of community college transfer students because of its own limited resources. Will community college leaders follow these trends and squeeze out those students whose only choice for a higher education lies with the community college but who have poor academic records and who do not know how to negotiate the higher education system? Certainly, who is admitted to community colleges, especially in light of today's economic situation, has a number of ethical dimensions.

Tensions always pull leaders in a number of directions. In responding to these tensions, leaders face ethical dilemmas that must be resolved in the context of the larger environment. How community college leaders resolve these dilemmas may well determine how well community colleges serve society in the future. One purpose of this chapter is to set the stage for the remainder of the book by placing the discussion in the perspective of the community college environment.

It seems desirable to define the word *ethics* early in the discussion, although readers should be aware that the authors of some other chapters provide their own definition of ethics or choose not to offer a definition. *Ethics,* as used here, is that set of principles, beliefs, and rules of moral conduct that guides the actions of the members of the college community. This definition fits well with the prevailing philosophy of most community college leaders: it is practical, not philosophical; it connotes action, not passivity; it involves not so much good versus evil as abiding by ethical standards of conduct (see Brockett, 1988, p. 2; Shea, 1988, pp. 15–21).

Some principles, beliefs, and rules of conduct may be incorporated into the faculty handbook in a statement on ethics governing all or part of the college community. On the other hand, many of the principles of ethical behavior may remain unwritten, for their vitality and usefulness result from their acceptance by a majority of the members of the college community and not from inclusion in a handbook that is rarely read other than by new members of the campus community or for occasional legal guidance. To be effective, an institution's commitment to ethical behavior, whether written or unwritten, must be in concert with the mission of the institution. Ethical behavior must be practiced by most members of the college community in such a way that, over time, it becomes an important part of the institution's culture. A central question that must be answered is, What can be done on our campuses to strengthen the commitment to ethical values?

In this chapter, I emphasize the role of the leader, especially the college president, in establishing a climate on campus that promotes ethical values. By introducing the president's role in setting the climate, I set the stage for Chapter Three, in which the author argues for a code of ethics to govern presidential behavior. I also argue that the successful leader ultimately goes beyond influencing institutional climate to influencing institutional culture. And I make some practical suggestions as to how ethical considerations can become an important part of the decision-making process on campus.

### Ethics and the Rule of Reason

Richard Nixon's weathered, pensive face graced the cover of the April 2, 1990, issue of *Time*. The issue's lead story consisted of excerpts from Nixon's book *In the Arena,* a work described on the cover of *Time* as an "emotional and extraordinarily candid memoir." In looking back at the Watergate scandal, Nixon laments, "In retrospect, while I was not involved in the decision to conduct the break-in, I should have set a higher standard for the conduct of the people who participated in my campaign and Administration. I should have established a moral tone that would have made such actions unthinkable. I did not. . . . Not taking a higher road than my predecessors and my adversaries was my central mistake" (Nixon, p. 38).

How do the issues that apply to the rough and tumble of Nixon's political arena apply to the civility and gentility of the academic stage? A federal judge recently ruled that Rutgers University was wrong in firing a professor accused of exploiting two Chinese scholars by making them work in his garden and do household chores. Why did the judge reverse the university's decision? Because, she said, the university's regulations governing faculty conduct did not specify that ethical lapses were grounds for dismissal. The judge acknowledged that a university's standards should allow for dismissal on ethical grounds but said that Rutgers's standards did not make such a provision. The blame, according to the judge, "lies squarely with the faculty, which has effectively blocked every attempt by the administration to beef up the dismissal standards" (Magner, 1990, p. A2).

The Rutgers case raises an interesting question: Must an institution of higher education spell out in a legal document or handbook its rules and regulations regarding what constitutes unethical conduct? Certainly, most institutions of higher education list in legal documents or handbooks a number of unacceptable behaviors, such as sexual or racial harassment, plagiarism, stealing, and other commonly agreed-upon ethical violations. Not many institutions have rules governing such things as using graduate students to do a professor's work, making noncredit courses credit courses to generate more state funds, allowing board members to act in their own interest rather than in the best interest of the institution, or any number of other practices that are questionable but that are difficult if not impossible to codify.

Should not a "rule of reason" apply (especially since our institutions of higher education represent themselves as citadels of reason)? The rule of reason assumes that members of the academic community can agree that the community's standards of right and wrong, its rules of ethical conduct, have been violated and that the wrongdoer must be punished for having breached the standards, perhaps even banned from membership in the community.

If rules and regulations alone are the sources of ethical standards, there is little hope that any institution anywhere can ever anticipate what the next violation of ethical conduct will be and cover the violation in the faculty handbook. For example, how many handbooks deal with the ethical considerations inherent in a highly visible, successful, and emotional head basketball coach venting his anger by throwing a chair across the college arena? On the other hand, if the rule of reason applies, colleges and universities can take the high ground and can set a moral tone that results in a standard of conduct that is understood and accepted by members of the academic community.

One of the problems in dealing with ethics on campus is that too few presidents, deans, and faculty members, or anyone else for that matter, are willing to step forward and say that on their campus, at this point in time, they are committed to ethical behavior and will not deliberately violate this stand or permit others to violate it without retribution. Throwing the first stone is difficult (in contrast to throwing the first chair), especially when everyone lives in a house at least partially constructed of glass. Furthermore, ethical values must constantly be subjected to critical analysis and revised when needed. Many ethical practices have been revised because perspectives on race and gender have changed.

If community college leaders are to avoid the ethical dilemmas that ensnare many of their colleagues, the campus climate must
be one in which ethical considerations are a part of the decision-
making process. Although talk of punishment is anathema to many
academics, they can nevertheless, while tolerating and indeed encouraging differences of opinion as to the specifics of rules and
regulations, agree on what constitutes unethical behavior. And they
must punish those who violate the rules, even their professional
colleagues.

How can leaders of community colleges weave the debate on
ethical issues into the fabric of campus activities and thus arrive at
practical solutions to the many ethical issues faced by members of
every campus community? Before exploring this question, a brief
discussion of ethics and higher education is in order.

## Ethics and Higher Education

Higher education, in general, has played its role of ethical arbitrator
rather well. Its leaders have generally taken the high road in dealing
with ethical behavior. However, leadership from the academic community in solving ethical issues at the national and international
levels has been scant, with the exception of leadership on a few "big
ticket" issues such as divestiture in South Africa. Nevertheless, for
every professor who misuses graduate students, there are hundreds
who give of themselves and of their knowledge in order that students may grow in wisdom and in stature. For every Nobel laureate
who has been caught plagiarizing, there are thousands of professors
who document their work to the smallest detail. For every "fusion
in a bottle" fiasco, researchers take giant strides in the search for a
cure for cancer.

Can leaders in higher education, then, be unconcerned with
ethical issues? Are the cases that make the headlines the only ones
requiring attention? No, for higher education today does not exist
in an ivory tower, if it ever did—certainly community colleges never
did. Academics are not immune to the temptations that afflict the
rest of society.

Higher education, then, has not ignored the need for maintaining ethical standards among its members, although there is lit-

tle evidence to suggest that these standards are universal or even accepted by much of the academic community. Nevertheless, in 1968, Eric Ashby, a master of Clare College in Cambridge, England, and former vice-chancellor of the University of Cambridge, called for a "Hippocratic oath" for the academic profession.

A decade later, Ashby noted that "at the moment there is no declared code of professional practice to which academics have subscribed. . . . If we had such a code, it would stabilize what I fear is a schizophrenic and disintegrating profession, and it would provide a basis of authority and example to the students" (1977, p. 273). Ashby's Hippocratic oath would require the scholar to subscribe to a rigorous code of ethics that would prohibit a blurring of the facts in any way, for scholarship, Ashby feels, has "an inherent morality" (p. 275).

Ashby offers advice that applies equally to all professionals, including community college leaders. He notes that often there are any number of conflicting views on what is good and what is bad for society. "Someone has to make a balanced judgment between these two sets of factors, and you can't make balanced judgments of values without working out your own sets of values" (1977, p. 282). Certainly, if community college presidents, trustees, and others are to promote ethical values on campus, they must work out their own sets of values and make balanced judgments among competing values, thus setting a moral tone that others will accept and emulate.

Clark Kerr, in a speech given at the twentieth anniversary meeting of Harvard University's Institute for Educational Management, picks up on Ashby's phrase "a disintegrating profession" in describing ethics and university teachers. Kerr (1989) notes that academics are quite willing to study ethics in general and are especially prone to write about medical and legal ethics. Kerr also notes the dearth of literature on academic ethics and believes that this lack of literature hinders the advancement of academic ethics. Indeed, Kerr could have turned to a report by Paul N. Ylvisaker, former dean of the Harvard Graduate School of Education, for support regarding the scarcity of literature on ethics in higher education. Ylvisaker studied 206 codes of ethics of various professions and discovered that while such fields as psychology and engineering have extensive codes of ethics, there is no generic code for educators (Ylvisaker, 1983, pp. 30-32).

Some segments of higher education have developed codes of ethics for some of their members. For example, in 1988, the American Association of State Colleges and Universities issued a policy statement entitled "Ethical Practices for College Presidents." In 1978, the Association of California Community College Administrators adopted a code called "Statement of Ethics: Professional Standards for Community College Administrators" (revised in 1981, 1986, and 1989). Currently, the Presidents Academy of the American Association of Community and Junior Colleges is considering a code of ethics for community college presidents. More will be said about this code in a subsequent chapter.

These codes, which some people see as a step in the right direction, nevertheless fail to provide an umbrella code (or generic code, to use Ylvisaker's phrase) of ethics covering all members of the college community. Indeed, if the codes are to become a part of an institution's culture, they must be incorporated into its mission statement, where they can serve as guideposts to ethical decision making rather than as inflexible boundaries that prescribe actions to be taken.

Joining the call for a code of ethics for academics, Kerr believes that such codes might be designated "derivative ethics" because they can only exist if they are effective. "They seek to set forth what each person should expect in the conduct of others, and what each person in return owes in his own conduct toward others, to make relations over the longer term more effective" (Kerr, 1989, p. 141). While pointing out that in the past higher education has handled its ethical responsibilities rather well, Kerr ends his discussion on a somewhat pessimistic note: "I conclude, regretfully, that the academic profession may, in fact, be disintegrating slowly in some aspects of its ethical conduct. I also conclude that the academic profession should not practice valuative neutrality about its own ethical values any more than should the medical or legal professions" (p. 156). Community college leaders who wish to create a campus climate and a culture that embrace and promote decision making based on accepted concepts of right and wrong and who promote institutional effectiveness and leadership simply cannot remain neutral on institutional values. As we argue, community college leadership has an ethical dimension.

Other academics also have commented on the need for academic leaders to be concerned with ethical values. Harold L. Enarson, president emeritus of Ohio State University, asks and answers the question, What are the ethical dimensions of a college or university presidency? Enarson, like Ashby and Kerr, bemoans the lack of concern for the ethical dimension of academic leadership. He believes that college and university presidents should operate according to consistent values applied consistently. For example, he believes that to define institutional purpose is to define the values of the organization, to manage an institution of higher education is to strive to ensure that administrative decisions reflect the values and mission of the institution, and to lead a college or university is to transform it over time so that it better reflects the values of society (Enarson, 1984, p. 25).

The test of integrity, Enarson believes, is whether or not the institution lives by its own rules. Enarson, after his many years in the administrative trenches, understands as only someone who has been there can understand that it is easy for presidents with good intentions and good character to look the other way as "subtle signs of corruption appear. . . . The avoidance of wrongdoing is, of course, the easiest of the moral imperatives. Indeed, this is the bare minimum required of leaders who prize both personal and institutional integrity. Beyond is the more important and difficult imperative of promoting the highest values of the institution, the self, and the society" (1984, p. 25). Enarson says that "there is not a single code of ethics to follow" (p. 26). Although Enarson is perhaps correct in his lament regarding the lack of a code of ethics, this problem does not alter the need for community college leaders to set a moral standard for the institution that is in concert with the institutional mission.

In addition to established leaders such as Enarson, Kerr, and Ashby, any number of institutions and higher education leaders are currently looking at the role of ethics in the curriculum. For example, reforms in college sports, although being made slowly, are nevertheless occurring.

The spring 1989 issue of *Educational Record,* published by

the American Council on Education, focuses on moral leadership in higher education. In one article, the president of an urban university discusses the role of the president in establishing a moral tone on campus. Another article discusses academic politics and presidential leadership. A higher education scholar entitles his article "The Moral Message of the University." In a similar vein, a community college dean of instruction entitled his remarks to a group of community college faculty members and administrators "Community Colleges and Civic Literacy: The Quest for Values, Ethics, and College Renewal." A community college faculty member examined ethics and administration in America's community colleges and concluded that community college administrators must define ethical standards of conduct for themselves and for future leaders if the community college is to serve its constituents (Whisnant, 1988).

Leaders in higher education, then, have not been blind to ethical issues, although, as Kerr points out, they have been reluctant to deal with these issues. It now seems to be the time for leaders in all segments of higher education to heed Kerr's advice (1988, p. 141) and "seek to set forth what each person should expect in the conduct of others, and . . . in return owes in his own conduct toward others." These leaders must realize that much that occurs on campus ultimately penetrates into society as graduates assume their roles as teachers, doctors, nurses, lawyers, legal assistants, business leaders, and technicians.

All leaders in higher education are subject to temptations. Community college leaders, positioned in that middle ground on the academic continuum where the community intersects with the college in ways not found in much of the rest of higher education and committed to serving all segments of society, are certainly no exception. Indeed, community college leaders are constantly subjected to the song of the Lorelei, ever luring them to cross the line of ethical misconduct only to be broken apart on rocks masquerading as easy solutions to ever-present funding and image problems.

Noting the almost blind commitment on the part of some community college leaders to achieving what they perceive to be the mission of their school, one community college faculty member reminds us that "the important note to keep in mind is that unethical behavior may not always be the result of an individual's quest for personal gain. Rather, unethical behavior may result from what the administrator views as institutionally necessary decisions or interpretations of policy" (Whisnant, 1988, p. 244).

One example serves to illustrate how blind adherence to the perceived mission of a college raises a number of ethical issues. In this situation, a community college was committed to serving the coal mining industry. The mining company required a flexible class schedule for its workers because they worked various shifts. The company preferred that classes be taught on site at company headquarters. One of the college's students—an employed miner—when asked whether he preferred to take classes on campus or at the mine site, responded that he preferred the classes held at the mine. (The purpose of the question was to determine if the miners took pride in coming to the campus and blending in with the other students.) When asked why he preferred to take classes at the mine, he replied that he got three more hours of credit with no additional work if he took the class at the mine site. Further questioning revealed that his work at the mine was viewed as a cooperative learning experience, although it required no additional work on his part.

What are the ethical implications inherent in this situation other than the obvious one of compromised academic integrity? First, the student has a distorted view of what should be required to obtain a college degree. Second, the image of the college from this student's perspective (and probably from a number of other perspectives) was one of "anything goes" rather than one of promoting ethical principles. Third, the college received funds from the state and tuition costs from the mining company for "void" college credits, a serious legal as well as ethical lapse. Fourth, the funding formula based upon student enrollment, not academic or fiscal integrity, was the driving force in the decision-making process of the leaders of the college. The decision to pad the enrollment figures was not an evil decision on the part of the college leadership; rather, it was a decision that did not take into consideration the ethical dimensions of leadership.

## Knowing When to Say No

Community college presidents, as is true with all leaders, must learn to say no to any number of requests but must do so without losing constituent support. Indeed, saying no is an art that the successful leader practices daily. But does the art of saying no have an ethical base?

The following brief case studies illustrate how three community college presidents said no and lived to lead another day. The first case is personal: the situation is as vivid in my memory today as it was on that day almost two decades ago when I stood in the office of the board chair and faced my first ethical dilemma as president. The second case describes a situation faced by James Hudgins, president of Midlands Technical College, and the third illustration comes from Richard Greenfield, current community college leader and former president of three community colleges, including the St. Louis Community College District.

### Case One

I had been in my first presidency for only three weeks (my spouse was still packing for the move) when I received a call from the board chair asking if I could come to his office for a brief meeting. Of course, I volunteered to meet with him at his convenience. His "convenience" was two hours after I received the call.

When I arrived at the chair's office, I was met by him and another member of the board. After we exchanged cordial greetings, the chair said, "Dr. Vaughan, here are the names of three people I want to see appointed to the college faculty."

Suddenly it all came back to me. The college was located in the most political section of the state: even the janitor's position at the courthouse in the chair's home district was up for grabs at election time, and the janitor regularly changed with a change in the party. How could I say no to a chair who lived and died by the political code of his district?

I took the three names and looked the board chair in the eye and said, "Thank you for the names. Let me assure you that they will get every consideration. If they come to the top of the stack they will be employed. If they don't, they won't. But I promise you one thing: the fact that you recommended them *will not* be held against them." I politely excused myself, returned to my motel, and called my wife. I suggested that she stop packing since I had probably concluded my tenure as president after an inglorious three weeks. As a new president, I had obviously not learned the art of saying no. I did, however, know where I had drawn my compromise line and was not about to cross it.

Thus my ethical dilemma was not in deciding whether to accept political appointments to the college faculty; I had decided long before becoming president that I would never do so. My ethical dilemma was in making sure that the three applicants favored by the chair were treated like all other applicants. As it turned out, I kept my promise while remaining true to myself. One of the three applicants was employed, an outstanding choice I should add, and the other two applicants lost out to more qualified candidates.

### Case Two

Midlands Technical College depends on two counties, Richland and Lexington, for its local budget. The local budget is approved by council members who are elected from single-member districts. During the previous four years, the college had enjoyed the support of a large majority of the eleven-member Richland County Council. One major exception was a council member who had strong negative feelings toward the college based on a bad experience with the college that occurred several years ago.

I visited him twice to seek a reconciliation between him and the college. He was courteous but refused the offer. During the previous two years, he had served as chair of the county council. On three occasions in 1990, he had used his authority to reduce or deny funding for the college.

In the fall of 1990, he was in a close race for his council seat. A member of his opponent's party informed a newspaper reporter that he had not acted in the best interest of education, especially Midlands Technical College. The reporter called me three days before the election and asked me to comment on the relationship between the council member and the college. I possessed information that would have been damaging to his campaign.

Although I personally opposed his candidacy and desired, for the benefit of the college, his defeat at the polls, I concluded that revealing this information in a time frame that would give him no opportunity to respond would not be ethical. I declined the request.

On the same weekend, I received a call from his opponent, a former student of the college who expressed his intent to support the college if elected. He offered me a similar opportunity to provide information damaging to his opponent. When I explained my intent to keep the college out of the political campaign and asked for his understanding, he courteously withdrew his request.

The story has a happy ending. The council member's challenger was elected, and since the campaign, he has reaffirmed his intention to support the college.

## Case Three

After years in the presidency, at least some incumbents realize that there are many roads to Jerusalem and that their ideas of right and wrong are not necessarily absolute. With age comes caution and a sense of relativity, tempered by a growing awareness of vulnerability and the need to protect one's flanks if one is to survive in the face of internal as well as external community pressures. After age fifty to fifty-five, few incumbent presidents can move readily into another presidency. For most, any shift to a "lesser" position, other than perhaps to a professorship at a university, signifies a great loss of status, a punctured ego, and consignment to limbo. Hence, at least some aging presidents may be willing to compromise their ethical standards in the interest of job security. Ironically, in doing so, they often undermine the very security that they seek since ultimately their weakness is perceived, and a compromised president frequently becomes a former president.

The case I relate occurred fairly early in my presidential career, while I was in my early forties. As founding president of a new community college, I was in the midst of building an entire campus as well as expanding the size of the faculty and support staff to meet surging demand and rapid growth in student enrollments. Blessed with an outstanding and prestigious appointed board of trustees, the college enjoyed great community support and experienced no overt political interference or attempts at improper influence during the first few years of its existence. Personnel and business decisions were made on the basis of appropriate criteria, policies, and procedures.

However, at some point, those people involved in local government, which sponsored the college and supported it with tax dollars, came to realize that they might be able to influence the appointment of staff or the awarding of contracts. I was contacted by a person who was very powerful in local politics and government and who had been a key supporter of the college in the course of its establishment and early development, including during the appointment of the blue-ribbon founding board of trustees. I was not asked to do anything illegal but was asked to consider certain people for appointments for various positions and to favor certain firms in making business decisions where bidding laws were not involved.

I was tempted to consider ways of pleasing this very powerful person and the forces he represented by cooperating, but I felt that personnel appointment policies and procedures had to be protected and business decisions had to be made on an impartial basis to foster the best interests of the college in the long run. At the same time, I was aware of the possibility that any refusal on my part could jeopardize this local support and perhaps my own job security.

I decided to have a private meeting with the person involved. At this meeting, I explained that the college would welcome inquiries or recommendations concerning any aspect of college operations from any source, but that as an appointed official with a public trust, I had to make sure that everyone, whether job applicant or vendor, would be treated impartially and fairly. Decisions would be made with the future of the college in mind and not with the idea of the college becoming a part of local government or local politics.

Of course, I was greatly concerned over his reaction to my views for the future of the college and myself. Fortunately, my reassurance of fair treatment and the genuine pride in the progress of the college exhibited by the official led him to back down and to agree that my decision (supported completely by the college's board of trustees) was one he could live with. He and his colleagues continued to be good supporters of the college in the years ahead and to refrain from attempting to control the operation of the institution.

### The Role of the President

The central question to be answered by this book is, What can be done on our campuses to strengthen the commitment to ethical values? This chapter introduces the question and provides some answers. The remaining chapters also deal with the question, and the concluding chapter offers a road map to ethical decision making.

I believe the answer to this question lies, in part, in the desire and ability of community college leaders to create a framework on campus in which ethical values can evolve and be examined, a framework that will result in a campus climate in which decisions are considered and made from the perspective of what is ethically right. Implicit in creating such a campus climate is the belief that the rules, regulations, and standards of conduct of the college must be in concert with the mission of the college.

Although it would be impossible and impractical to codify accepted ethical behavior for all possible situations or decisions on campus, it is possible to create at least a basic code or pattern of behavior. This "code of integrity," if you will, should bind all members of the academic community and hold them responsible for their behavior and decisions. And although all members of an academic community may not be able to agree upon set rules and regulations regarding ethical behavior, one would hope that they could distinguish between ethical and unethical behavior, between acting with integrity and acting dishonorably. If people in the college community view decisions from the perspective of ethical behavior, the campus climate evolves to the point where ethical considerations become a part of the culture of the institution, a culture with roots in the past that extend into the future. I believe that institutional decisions based on those ethical values that are in concert with the college mission will effectively meet societal, institutional, and individual needs by maintaining integrity in all aspects of the college's operation.

Who should take the lead in establishing a climate on campus based upon accepted concepts of right and wrong? I believe the leader in this goal must be the college president. Just as Nixon had the responsibility to set the moral climate for his administration, so the president of a college has the responsibility for setting the moral climate for the campus. However, community college presidents cannot and should not act alone in establishing and maintaining this campus climate.

The president occupies a unique position on campus and is the person with the greatest potential to see that members of the campus community take ethics seriously. The president is the person most likely to influence the campus climate and ultimately the campus culture. And the president is the one person on campus who cannot say, "Ethical behavior at this institution is not my problem." The final responsibility for ethics does indeed rest with the president, whether the president chooses to promote ethical conduct or run the risk of ignoring ethical misconduct.

Community college presidents must not fail, as Nixon did with the White House, to set a moral tone on campus that causes members of the college community to think, judge, and act with integrity. To fail to set this moral tone is to court the disaster that ultimately befalls leaders in our society who violate the rules. These leaders limit their own accomplishments and the accomplishments of those they are morally bound to lead. If U.S. democracy and its proud offspring, our higher education system, are to be successful, leaders at all levels must be able to distinguish right from wrong, to act on what is right, and to deal with breaches of ethical conduct.

### Ethics and Institutional Culture

In literally thousands of conversations with community college leaders, I have rarely heard anyone discuss institutional culture. Institutional cultures evolve over many years and sometimes over several centuries and are often documented, in part, in extensive institutional histories. When this long-term evolution is contrasted with the short history of community colleges (most community college histories consist of a page in the college catalogue), one can understand why institutional culture has rarely been a topic of discussion among community college leaders at professional meetings, in the literature, or on campus.

In a parallel argument, and one that supports the need to make ethics a part of the community college culture, one author argues that the brief history of the community college increases the chances that community college administrators will make ethically questionable decisions. Pointing out that most community colleges are less than three decades old, the author notes, "This stage of development means that the community college does not have a reserve of experience or tradition from which to draw in times of difficult decision making. Community college administrators do not have generations of predecessors having left a legacy to follow" (Whisnant, 1988, p. 246). Whether having a legacy on which to base their ethical decisions would enhance the ability of community college administrators to make ethical decisions is debatable. What is not debatable is that all organizations, including community colleges, have a culture (Birnbaum, 1988; Kuh and Whitt, 1988). If community colleges are to serve as an important avenue for promoting ethical behavior, consistent ethical conduct must become a recognized part of their institutional culture.

How can institutional culture be used to promote rules of conduct based on a standard of ethics? Perhaps before answering this question, we should examine institutional culture and its relationship to the community college.

Definitions of the term *institutional culture* abound. Kuh and Whitt (1988) note that over thirty-five years ago, two scholars reported 164 different definitions of culture. Peterson and his colleagues point out that ambiguity exists regarding what constitutes organizational culture and note that "the definition of organizational culture is neither precise nor consensual" (Peterson and others, 1986, p. 11). They believe that the attributes of culture—values, beliefs, and assumptions—distinguish the concept of culture from the concept of climate. They observe that the institutional climate consists of individual attitudes and perceptions and that these may change much more quickly than the values, beliefs, and assumptions that make up the institutional culture. The distinction between climate and culture is relevant to this discussion and will be alluded to below.

Culture grows out of past and present actions (process) and results in shared values, beliefs, and assumptions about an institution (product). Institutional image and culture have a symbiotic relationship; one constantly feeds and shapes the other.

Institutional culture changes slowly. For example, outmoded attitudes toward race have dominated the culture of some institutions, outmoded attitudes toward religion others, and outmoded attitudes toward gender still others. The domination of these attitudes often inhibits the development of students and faculty members whose values are in conflict with the existing culture.

Although understanding a culture is a rational process, appreciating an institution's culture can be an emotional process, one that demands sensitivity to what has gone before and what may happen in the future. This sensitivity often evokes chills and even tears when one sings a certain song or visits a certain place on campus. Culture consists of those things that make an institution distinct: its history, traditions, values, interaction with the larger environment, ceremonies, renewal process—including recruitment and selection of personnel—and evaluation process, including assessment of its ethical values.

Any discussion of institutional culture raises a number of questions. Do members of the college community generally agree upon concepts of ethical behavior and integrity to such a degree that these concepts are an inherent part of the institutional culture? Or is the culture one that says "anything goes," for example, winning football games at any cost or padding enrollment figures in order to generate full-time-equivalent students (FTEs)? Is the culture one that encourages, indeed rewards, taking a stand on institutional values? Is the culture in tune with the times, especially in relationship to women and minorities, both on campus and in society? How do we know when to let parts of our culture die or when to kill them?

Open access, an important aspect of the culture of a community college, is itself a value statement. Admitting students who have academic deficiencies and not dealing with those deficiencies, however, is ethically wrong. Myths, legends, and stories of the founding of the college and of early institutional leaders are part of institutional culture; they contribute to a sense of history and community and inspire loyalty to the institution. The culture of an institution influences how the institution is perceived by members of the college community and by the community at large.

The effective leader understands and is sensitive to the culture of an institution. The leader respects and preserves the good things of the past but always leads in shaping the present and planning for the future. The effective leader, and especially the effective president, understands when and where to try to change an institution's culture and when to let go of past values that are no longer acceptable in society or as a part of the institutional mission. The effective leader discusses the institutional culture in ways that can be understood by much of the public, often using metaphors with which the audience identifies. Indeed, the highly successful president becomes one with the culture, as its interpreter and as the symbol of the institution. The president absorbs and is absorbed by the institutional culture and ultimately becomes an integral part of that culture, often after passing from the scene.

The importance of leaders, especially presidents, in influencing the campus climate and ultimately shaping institutional culture helps to answer in part the question posed earlier: what can be done on our campuses to strengthen the commitment to ethical values? The answer, in the broadest sense, is that the president and other campus leaders working with the governing board can shape the institutional culture in ways that assure that members of the college community examine and live by the rules and values of the college and that these rules and values are instilled as a permanent part of the campus culture.

## Actions for Shaping Institutional Culture

Changing the culture of an institution is extremely difficult and somewhat risky if the changes depart dramatically from accepted and revered practices. Nevertheless, changing the culture of the institution is an important way for community college leaders to shape institutional values.

Assuring that ethical values occupy a prominent role in the

decision-making process on campus should not rend the cultural fabric of most campuses or even be seen as a challenge to the existing culture. Rather, by emphasizing values in the decision-making process and by encouraging members of the college community to ask if a decision or an act is right or wrong, community college leaders tap into those institutional values normally associated with effective institutions of higher education. Therefore, the leaders are not perceived as inventing or imposing new values. They can subtly but effectively change the institutional culture without creating chaos or hostility among members of the college community.

In the rest of this section, I offer suggestions for shaping the culture of a community college in ways that enhance the commitment of the institution to doing the right thing, regardless of the issue at hand. The suggestions take into consideration that each institution is unique and has its own unique culture.

A first, and perhaps most important, step for shaping the culture of institutions based on ethical values is for presidents to be sensitive to the ethical dimension of leadership. Once presidents step forward and insist that decisions be made from an ethical base, students, faculty members, staff members, and trustees will be more inclined to view their roles from the perspective of ethical behavior or at least to think about and perhaps debate the ethical dimensions of their decisions. All members of the college community can then sense that the campus climate is one in which debating of ethical issues is valued and encouraged. Thus the process of placing ethics at the center of the campus culture begins. It is at this point that the president begins to influence the campus climate in a positive way, at least as far as placing emphasis upon institutional values (influencing the culture takes longer).

How can presidents bring an ethical dimension to their leadership without giving the appearance of having just descended from Mount Sinai, hoisting high a faculty handbook filled with rules and regulations, the breaking of which will bring forth harsh moral judgments? This is very difficult. But effective presidents realize that a sure way to alienate the college community is to become preachy or moralistic, regardless of whether the subject is conserving energy, serving students, or maintaining ethical standards.

Probably the most effective way for presidents to bring an

ethical approach to their leadership is to be above reproach in their own professional and personal actions. It is good to remember that the incumbent is president twenty-four hours a day, seven days a week, three hundred and sixty-five days a year. Serving as a role model extends into the president's personal life in ways not experienced by other members of the college community, and few things are off limits when considering the conduct of the president. By serving as an example of good ethical conduct, the president becomes a role model and symbol for other members of the college community. Leading by example, then, is the first step presidents can take to establish a climate on campus that embraces values built upon a sense of right and wrong.

Next, presidents must use the many opportunities available almost daily to exhibit ethical behavior, thereby weaving their own behavior into the fabric (and ultimately the culture) of the institution. The president may present day-to-day issues and problems that are ethical dilemmas to the college community and ask for help in finding a resolution that is in concert with the values of the institution. Ethical decision making thus becomes a part of the daily activities of the campus. As one president, my friend and colleague Robert Templin, is fond of saying, by using current situations to emphasize ethics, the president is a "teacher and not a preacher."

Once the president engages in a decision-making process based upon the accepted values of the institution, and especially if other members of the campus are involved, the college community can reflect upon the actions taken. By "doing ethics" the president can encourage all members of the college community to discuss the ethical dimensions of leadership and decision making. The discussions may, however, become little more than philosophical wanderings that devour a great deal of time and energy but yield few useful results, especially if no mechanism is available to test ethical concepts in a way that produces a product.

To provide an anchor for the discussions and to encourage a product at the end of the process, the president should build discussions around applying ethical practices to existing issues. For example, one approach might be for members of a campus community to examine the rules and regulations governing the college and to use this examination to focus the debate on values. They might ask, Are the rules fair? Do any of them discriminate against women or ethnic or racial minorities? Although few members of the college community are interested in discussing rules and regulations in isolation, using rules and regulations as the bridge to a discussion of ethics in a broader context might be useful on some campuses.

Once the discussion on the fairness of rules and regulations has served its purpose, the more difficult question of whether the rules and regulations are applied consistently and fairly to all members of the college community can lead the discussion of ethics to a higher level. The discussion of rules and regulations may generate a list of issues that a later definition or later concepts of ethics can be applied to or tested against.

A similar but more interesting and creative way of broaching the subject of ethics on a community college campus is one used at Brookdale Community College. After polling members of the campus community regarding what they viewed as ethical concerns on campus, campus leaders held a series of nine seminars to discuss the issues. Using case studies based upon real situations at the college (past or present), the organizer of the seminars assigned various roles to those who were willing to act out the cases. No attempt was made to find the right answers; rather, "the participants came up with a set of tentative guidelines to distinguish morally acceptable from morally unacceptable behavior" (Mellert, 1990, p. 1). All the participants thought the discussions were worthwhile, and those in attendance learned from the process and were able to relate the ethical issues discussed to their own campus responsibilities.

Once members of the campus community have discussed ethics and have had time to reflect and to draw some conclusions about what is meant by the ethical dimensions of leadership, the governing board of the college must be actively brought into the process. The board should be aware of the debates taking place on campus regarding ethics, especially if rules and regulations are being examined. If the institutional culture is to reflect ethical values, the board must be involved in both the processes and products that will shape that culture. The board should be brought into the process carefully, for the board members must not see themselves as arbitrators for ethical conduct. On the other hand, the board has a right and responsibility to help determine campus values.

At this stage, the president can exert leadership in helping the board members to understand their role in assuring ethical conduct among themselves and among members of the college community. (In working with the board, the president's role must once again be to teach and not preach.) The board members must, however, avoid taking a moralistic stance, especially in raising questions related to activities that have little to do with how individuals perform as board members or as members of the college community. They must resist the temptation to peek into the personal lives of individuals. (Here, again, the president is something of an exception.) The board members should thoroughly discuss the meaning of the terms *institutional ethics* and *institutional culture,* yet resist the temptation to offer an official definition of either at this stage. But the board should make clear its interest in helping shape the institution's understanding of ethics and should recognize that the ultimate goal is to make ethics an even more important part of the culture of the college.

Once the board and president agree on the direction the discussion of the ethical dimensions of leadership should take in general, a committee should be established consisting of representatives from the board and from all segments of the college community. The committee's task and deadline should be clearly defined. For example, the committee may be asked to define ethics in the context of the institutional mission within six months.

The committee should be charged with applying the rule of reason when discussing its task because, again, not all statements of ethical behavior can or should be listed in the policy manual. Rather, the committee can propose a framework for discussing ethical values or, as at Brookdale Community College, establish a set of guidelines to distinguish morally acceptable from morally unacceptable behavior. A way of keeping the president involved and of assuring support from that office is to have the president chair the committee and present the report of the committee to both the board and to the college community.

All members of the college community and all members of the governing board should have the opportunity to debate the issues raised in the report and to offer recommendations for revision. The committee should then revise its report based upon the recommendations and submit the report to the governing board (assuming the president chairs the committee) with a recommendation for adoption.

The governing board should then issue its statement on ethics as official college policy. The statement should provide for periodic review and revision as required, for as Enarson (1984, p. 26) reminds us, "there is not a single code of ethics to follow," and there certainly is not one code for all people for all times. The college community should then apply the ethical principles to the daily activities of the college, incorporating appropriate portions of the policy statement into all publications, including the college catalogue, recruitment brochures, course syllabi, the annual report, fundraising material, and other appropriate publications.

## Conclusion

This chapter, in setting the stage for the remainder of the book, has attempted to offer some practical advice for incorporating into the institutional culture standards of ethical conduct that are understood and accepted by members of the academic community. Although I do not call for a formal code of ethical conduct as advocated by Ashby and others (a topic that will be dealt with more fully in a later chapter), I believe that if the culture of an institution incorporates debates on standards of right and wrong, the culture will ultimately be shaped by the debates. And thus the community of the institution will be more willing to take a stand on ethical issues and may issue a formal statement, approved by the governing board, that outlines the stand of the college on the ethical dimensions of leadership. The statement should follow a rule of reason rather than attempt to answer all ethical (and legal) questions for all times.

As Ylvisaker (1983) observes, "We arrive at an ethical decision and what ethics are, not by power, not by politics, not by the market mechanism . . . and not by compromise, but by some moral touchstone that is not identical with the law, nor even a code of ethics, or religion, or custom. It's a standard that is constantly evolving. There's a growth in our consciousness of what is ethical behavior. It's a sense that drives us to want to act nobly, to act in the general interest as well as in our own" (p. 31). Once the college community commits itself to a decision-making process based upon ethical values and applies these values in the general interest of all concerned, the college will be well on its way to creating a culture that inculcates these values and that judges its processes and products based upon these values.

## References

Ashby, E. "A Hippocratic Oath for the Academic Profession." In G. R. Urban (ed.), *Hazards of Learning*. La Salle, Ill.: Open Court, 1977.

Birnbaum, R. *How Colleges Work: The Cybernetics of Academic Organization and Leadership*. San Francisco: Jossey-Bass, 1988.

Brockett, R. G. "Ethics and the Adult Educator." In R. G. Brockett (ed.), *Ethical Issues in Adult Education*. New York: Teachers College, Columbia University, 1988.

Enarson, H. L. "The Ethical Imperative of the College Presidency." *Educational Record*, Spring 1984, pp. 24-26.

Kerr, C. "The Academic Ethic and University Teachers: A 'Disintegrating Profession'?" *Minerva*, Summer–Fall 1989, pp. 139-156.

Kuh, G. D., and Whitt, E. J. *The Invisible Tapestry: Culture in American Colleges and Universities*. Washington, D.C.: ERIC Clearinghouse for Higher Education, George Washington University, 1988.

Magner, D. K. "Can't Fire Professor for Ethical Lapses, Rutgers Told." *Chronicle of Higher Education*, Aug. 15, 1990, p. A2.

Mellert, R. B. "Ethics in Higher Education." *Innovation Abstracts*, 1990, *12*(30), 1-2.

Nixon, R. "I Could See No Reason to Live." *Time*, Apr. 2, 1990, pp. 34-49.

Peterson, M. W., and others. *The Organizational Context for Teaching and Learning: A Review of the Literature*. Ann Arbor: University of Michigan Press, 1986.

Shea, G. F. *Practical Ethics*. New York: American Management Association, 1988.

Whisnant, W. T. "Ethics and Administration in America's Community Colleges." *Community/Junior College Quarterly of Research and Practice*, 1988, *12*(3), 243-249.

Ylvisaker, P. N. "Ethical Problems in Higher Education." *AGB Reports*, Jan.-Feb. 1983, pp. 28-35.

# Chapter Two

# The Fear of Knowing
and the Ethics of Ignoring

## Arthur M. Cohen

Questions of ethics have been raised periodically regarding all of higher education. For decades, various commentators have deplored the tendency of universities to reward faculty members more highly for doing research than for teaching. Universities have been challenged on their participation in weapons research and their discriminatory admissions practices. Allegations have been made concerning inflation of student graduation and employment rates. Recently, the charge has been put forth that universities exploit their athletes, using them to support multimillion-dollar admissions fees and television contracts while not taking sufficient pains to ensure that they graduate.

If this chapter were about universities, it would not lack for concern about institutional ethics. In addition to the contentions stated above, it would examine the ethics of fundraising by asking, When does cultivation of a donor become dishonest manipulation? Should the university accept gifts with strings attached? It would take on the pseudoresearch in the social sciences and humanities, where researchers have attempted unsuccessfully to imitate the physical sciences, often with ludicrous effect. It would question the extent to which the focus on research weakens the instructional component of a university. And it would question the outcome of higher education because, except in the professional schools where students' entry into and progress in the professions is carefully tracked, universities are not among the standard bearers in defining the outcomes of their ministrations. But that critique is for a different work. This chapter is about community colleges.

How can the ethical dimensions of community colleges be viewed? Certainly any educational structure that opens its doors to all, grants absolution for previous academic sins, and assists people in rising above their station is righteous. But those are overriding purposes, general aims. Morality is a multilevel concept. What happens when we look into the specifics of institutional functioning?

Although few serious scholars have been concerned with community colleges, some have raised questions of institutional ethics. Karabel (1972, 1986) has repeatedly charged the colleges with unethically tracking their students along class-based lines. He and a colleague (Brint and Karabel, 1989) recently alleged that this tracking has been deliberate. Orfield (1984) charged the large-city colleges with perpetuating segregation. Zwerling (1976) attempted to document how community colleges channel their lower-class students into lower-class occupations. Pincus (1986) concluded that despite persistent claims to the contrary, "there is no good evidence that vocational education in community colleges delivers on the promise of secure employment, decent pay, and ample career opportunities" (p. 49).

This chapter considers a more subtle view of community college ethics than the ones posed by Karabel and his confrères. It seeks a perspective on the guiding ethos of the institution. What myths govern its practices? What images do its leaders promulgate? How are the values of the institution reflected in what the staff members say or in the data they collect?

Gordon, Miller, and Rollock (1990) use the term *communicentricity* to examine the ways in which knowledge is generated. They define communicentric bias as "the tendency to make one's

own community the center of the universe and the conceptual frame
that constrains all thought." Thus, a communicentric bias "not
only frames the conceptual paradigms we use to study social phe-
nomena, but also frames the methodological paradigms as well"
(p. 15). The authors conclude that knowledge is relative to the context in which it is generated. By this definition, the way the colleges
are seen by their staff members offers a more valid view of the
guiding principles of community colleges than the analyses provided by the few external commentators.

I will trace the communicentricity of community colleges
here by analyzing the communications emanating from them.
Much of what the colleges do remains unreported. (Community
college leaders often say, "We don't have time to write.") But several
journals are devoted exclusively to papers about community colleges. The ERIC Clearinghouse for Junior Colleges has abstracted
and catalogued some 13,000 college-generated documents in its
twenty-five-year history. There is a body of published literature pertaining to community colleges. And there are ephemera: presentations to conferences, opening-day-of-school speeches, professional
association newsletters, and so on. A group practicing its profession
leaves tracks.

## The Literature

The level of discourse in the literature on the colleges varies, depending on the purposes and audiences for which the articles are
written or to whom the presentations are made. A small portion of
the literature, 10 percent at most, is carefully documented. It is based
on reliable data and valid definitions, and its conclusions are reasonable. The practitioners who prepare this literature are administrators, faculty members, or institutional researchers in single
colleges; data compilers in district offices; or officials of state agencies. But because this literature represents such a small part of the
writings that emanate from the institutions, it is inadequate to
answer most questions of college functioning; journalists, public
officials, and others who seek consistent information on college
operations and effects cannot gain an adequate perspective from

this literature. Moreover, and more to the point of this chapter, this literature does not reflect the dominant institutional ethos.

Most of the literature that speaks of the colleges rests on a different foundation. One form is the public relations statement that is designed to convince unsophisticated audiences within and outside the colleges of the merits of the colleges. These common reports present discrete "good" information about the college, such as a student's winning a bird-whistling contest, a baseball team's winning a state title, a new program's retraining of unemployed female lumberjacks.

Another form of discourse centers on the uncoordinated tabulation of data such as the students' age, gender, and census tract of residence or the grade point averages of students who have been through day classes as opposed to evening classes. These data are readily obtainable from college records and easily manipulated. They are often compiled to satisfy external agencies and rarely are analyzed for their implications. State-level groups sometimes report such data in the aggregate.

College staff members also produce reports that evaluate programs or documents designed to justify funding that establishes or continues special curricula. When this literature is produced by the managers of the programs, as it often is, it reflects a bias toward program maintenance. College administrators who feel that it is important to keep the staff apprised of anticipated national economic and demographic shifts sometimes produce reports of extramural trends that could eventually affect their college.

The literature includes the results of many surveys asking, for example, how the students liked their experiences at the college. These surveys are often written by community college personnel who are enrolled in graduate programs at neighboring universities and who present these types of data to satisfy degree requirements.

To summarize, most of the literature reports disparate events that reflect positively on the college, tabular data drawn from college records, program or funding justifications, data about trends, or survey findings. The rare comprehensive analyses that do appear in the literature, such as those done by Weis in the study *Between Two Worlds* (1985), Richardson, Fisk, and Okun in *Literacy in the Open-Access College* (1983), or London in *The Culture of a Com-*

*munity College* (1978), are written by scholars who are not affiliated with community colleges.

The literature of community colleges provides two insights into institutional communicentricity. The first can be discerned by reviewing the documents in which the colleges' promoters, in their zeal to present the colleges favorably and thus sustain support, go beyond the bounds of rational discourse. The second analyzes the literature as a whole to draw inferences about the belief systems, values, guiding principles—in brief, the ethics—of the colleges.

### Literature That Goes Beyond the Bounds of Rationality

> Not only do we uphold the highest standards of quality. We stand behind our product.
>
> Our brand delivers consistent quality and flavor in every cigarette, in every pack, in every carton.
>
> We stand behind our product. You're smoking the best cigarette in America.
>
> So if you'd like to tell us how you feel about our cigarettes, just give us a call, toll free. You'll find the number on every pack and carton of our brand.

We expect inflated rhetoric from advertisers who are trying to create the illusion that they care for the public. There is nothing unethical about the above advertising. It may be illogical and it certainly is meaningless, because it offers no suggestion that the company will make redress. But we accept the statements because we know what the advertiser is trying to do. We do not seek a connection between the claim of high standards and the toll-free telephone number. We recognize the advertising as a blatant attempt to purvey an image of concern.

Most of the documents emanating from community colleges are similarly benign. They may seek to aggrandize the institution, but the worst charge that can be leveled at them is that they are promotional pieces and should be so judged. Occasionally, though, the pieces stretch the boundaries of rationality.

Bender analyzed some of the "unethical, false advertising" community colleges produced in their efforts to recruit students

(1975, p. 39). Many of the publications that he examined discussed the careers that graduates could enter and the money they would earn, with no comment on the programs' entry restrictions or retention rates. Some pieces boasted of the unique environment of the college or its quality of education, with no attempt at defining those terms. Bender concluded that in many cases Federal Trade Commission guidelines were being violated.

A different type of excess shows up in some of the studies designed to extol the benefits of the colleges. The economic-impact studies, for example, invariably find a positive effect because the colleges draw most of their funds from outside their service area while most of their beneficiaries, the students and staff members, reside within the locality. Therefore, a net cash benefit is guaranteed a priori, and the writers can readily manipulate the data and present bar graphs, tables, and pie charts to demonstrate how the funds flow through the community.

When writers seek to quantify the indirect benefits of community colleges, they sometimes reach strange conclusions. An economic-impact study done at Long Beach City College provides a case in point (Littlefield, 1982). After reviewing the flow of state funds into the local area, the author referred to impacts that "cannot be readily quantified. . . . Suppose there are 1,000 male high school graduates. Five and a half percent, or 55, would have been unemployed. . . . If these 55 enroll in a community college, we would expect their unemployment rate to drop to 4.2 percent after graduation. The number unemployed would thus drop from 55 to 3, a 95 percent reduction" (p. 45). A comparable calculation found a 95 percent reduction in the number of families receiving public assistance (p. 50). The author also concluded that the total student body would have a "total annual income increase" of $45,600,000, since people who have been to college earn considerably more than people who have not been to college and since 16,000 people attend the college (p. 37). And, because 94 percent of the prison population had not been to college, the author concludes that the community was saving an additional $18,000 per student per year, the difference between keeping a person in college or in jail.

A similar form of boundless reportage may emanate from community college associations. The following piece is reprinted in its entirety from the August 1, 1989, issue of *Community, Technical and Junior College Times*, published by the American Association of Community and Junior Colleges: "Students transferring from a community college to a University of California campus have a better shot at completing their baccalaureate degree than those who began their freshman year at a UC college, according to a new report by the university system. Of students who entered the University of California by transferring from a state community college, one-third graduated within two years and 70% graduated within four years. Of the students who entered the University of California as freshmen, 59% had graduated within five years. When looked at over a ten year period, some 65% of the students had graduated" ("Transfers Succeed . . . ," p. 1).

Individual college presidents also sometimes let their chauvinism lead them to utter uncomplimentary half-truths. The editorial page of the August 15, 1991, *Los Angeles Times* carried an article entitled "Save Undergrads from the Maw of UC" (Moore, 1991) that was written by the president of a community college. The president made several undocumented assertions, including the statement that the University of California, "having accepted only the 'brightest and best' high school graduates, organizes them into huge classes (200 to 1500 students), sends in graduate assistants to teach and then graduates only 54% of these students five years later" (p. B7).

The reports that cross the bounds of reason tell us something about the institutions that produce them. The verbiage in brochures is a form of advertising, harmless because it is obviously promotional; the Federal Trade Commission has more to do than to concern itself with college-generated flyers. The economic-impact studies are also flagrant propaganda pieces, but because they are reported in the garb of scholarly research and often distort that medium unconscionably, they represent egregious breaches of ethics.

The most distressing aspect of the study cited from *College Times* is that its conclusions made headlines in the newsletters of the state education association. They were repeated as though they were revealed truths. The comparison of the time to graduation of freshmen entering the university with the time to graduation of students entering as juniors after completing their lower-division work at a community college was similarly well received. No one mentioned the fact that more of the transfer students graduated because most students who drop out do so in their first two years, or that the transfer students graduated sooner than the freshmen because they had a two-year head start.

Similarly, the college president's gratuitous comments about the failings of the University of California in the *Los Angeles Times* included nothing about the number of huge classes that he deplored (actually less than .5 percent of the university's lower-division offerings) or about the percentage of students at the university who graduate after six or seven years. And he neglected to mention the class size and graduation rate in his own college.

Why are these types of reports accepted? The same answer applies to the self-congratulatory response to the fantastic conclusions of the economic-benefit study at Long Beach City College and to the benign acceptance of the half-truths of the transfer study in *College Times:* they make the community colleges look good. That is the primary critical standard, not whether the statement is valid, truthful, or accurate or would stand up to scrutiny.

How many college presidents have ever said to their institutional research directors or program heads, "Even though that report makes us look good, you must add a disclaimer regarding the limitations of the data and statistics on which it is based"? How many, on the other hand, have reacted with outrage to newspaper stories titled "Two-Year Colleges Fail Test" or "Community Colleges a 'Dead End' for Minorities"? Since self-serving reports and attention-grabbing headlines alike are often based on inaccurate data, creative statistics, and flawed conclusions, the ethics of responsible stewardship would suggest that college leaders apply a single standard to both. But, obviously, they do not.

## Literature That Promotes an Image

Do students succeed at our college? Let me tell you about Mildred.

When Mildred came to us, she was a twenty-seven-year-old, unemployed, illiterate single parent of

four who wanted to better herself and to get off the
welfare rolls. We worked with her, taught her to read,
and kept her children in our day-care center. She
passed her classes and transferred to the university,
where she's now a pre-med about to graduate with
honors.

You bet our students succeed!

In 1964, Daniel Boorstin published *The Image,* a book that popu-
larized the term *pseudo-event.* The pseudo-event is one that is designed for the immediate purpose of being reported, one that may
have an ambiguous relationship to the underlying reality of the
situation. Boorstin points out the centrality of the making of illusions, not only in advertising, public relations, and politics but also
in journalism, merchandising, and publishing—where the inter-
view and the news release are more important than any actual document delineating the issues or reporting the data. Boorstin says
that the making of illusions is not a matter of lies versus truths.
Rather, it involves the construction of persuasive statements that are
neither true nor false. The journalists, merchandisers, and public
servants who give us these illusions are honest. They are giving us
what we want: "a world where fantasy is more real than reality,
where the image has more dignity than its original" (Boorstin, 1964,
p. 37). Pseudo-events are more attractive than reality because true
experience is necessarily complicated.

Communication and the production of knowledge proceed
within common frames of reference. Educational researchers typically use social science research paradigms, in which the surveys
must be based on carefully drawn samples of the population, high
response rates, checks on bias of nonrespondents, questions that
have been pretested, and statistical analysis. The data in quantita-
tive and qualitative studies alike must be gathered according to
valid definitions, and the conclusions drawn are presumed to be
consistent with the data. Verification is vital.

However, even though nearly all community college faculty
members and administrators have been to graduate schools where
they learned research methods, few connect research with practice.
Those who are enrolled in graduate programs in neighboring uni-

versities often operate in two opposing ways simultaneously: they collect their data and write their papers using social science research methods to satisfy their university professors even while they are writing reports that extol their institutions without using those same methods of inquiry. They know how to conduct studies using these methods, but the research paradigms are too much at variance with the flow of information within their colleges.

Community college personnel may conduct surveys with little attendance to the canons of educational research. Ambiguous questions and low response rates from self-selected samples are acceptable. But the purposes for which the surveys are conducted are different and one set, one way of conducting them, cannot reasonably be used for the other purpose. The probabilities and estimates that social science research yields are weak forces compared to the guiding images of the colleges. And they seem even weaker when their analysis of variance, regression analysis, and other statistical baggage is juxtaposed with the public relations imperative and decision-making patterns of the colleges. The need for and the process of image making are paramount.

Why should community college practitioners use social science research models? Their values are not served by these models. Even though it is as easy to organize studies that meet the standards of social science research as it is to conduct studies less rigorously, most information seekers at community colleges ignore research criteria. Sampling students to enhance the reliability of data is rightfully neglected when the primary purpose of a survey is to bring the name of the college to the attention of the maximum number of current, former, and potential students; to show these people that the college cares about them; and to entice them to enroll. Tracking down the nonrespondents can be undertaken desultorily, if at all, when the audience for the report is uncritical. The studies may be cast in the research format, but they are not designed to add to a knowledge base. A question of ethics can be posed: Is the institution obligated to strive for reliable data before it releases information?

### Lack of Reliable Data

Few community college staff members seem concerned about the paucity of reliable data in their literature. The idea that they are exempt from scholarship by virtue of where they work has a long history. The contention that they are teachers and not researchers has persisted even though the colleges long ago severed their connection with the K-12 system.

Other institutional characteristics, funding patterns, for example, play a part in the lack of reliable data. Research offices at community colleges are severely understaffed. Twenty-five years ago, only one college in five had a formally organized research office. More recently, California community colleges reported less than one full-time research officer each, this in a state where the median college enrolls more than 8,000 students (Wilcox, 1987). Reimbursement schedules also contribute to the problem. In most states, colleges receive payment for the student who takes English 101 in the fall and for the student who takes English 102 in the spring. Whether those two enrollments represent the same student or two different students is immaterial. Therefore, staff members have no incentive to track the flow of students. The way that the records in most colleges are arrayed reflects this characteristic.

The bias toward cross-sectional data arrays is intensified by another characteristic: the importance of *not* knowing. The institutional spokesperson who is uneasy about the potentially negative interpretation of student-flow data may not want to know the proportion of students who transfer, graduate, get jobs, become literate, or attain great personal satisfaction as a result of attending the college. People may use this information to make untoward comparisons with selective-entry colleges, the information may make colleges in higher socioeconomic districts look better than others, or people who do not understand the unique mission of a school may look unkindly at its dropout rate. Budgets are formed in a political environment, and public support is sustained with images. Community college personnel may feel that it is best not to give out numbers that can be turned to the disadvantage of a school, that it is best not to know.

There are many ways of not knowing. One can release as few reliable data as possible, denying all but officially mandated requests. One can conceal the flawed data-collection process within the shell of educational research paradigms. One can publicize unique successes (cases like Mildred's) in the absence of representative commonalities. It is then but a short step onto the slippery slope of dishonesty in communication, where communication may be honest by the tenets of advertising, of purveying images, but not worthy of an educational structure. To be ignorant is to not know. To ignore facts is to know, but to deny. Neither approach is necessary, and both are unethical.

Community college staff members should not welcome the pseudo-images that dominate the transmission of information about their institution. The managers of public agencies who think that public opinion is molded by television news spots conclude that they are acting rationally when they release nothing but positive reports. But a continual drumroll of unsubstantiated information has several untoward effects. It blocks the collection of data that reflect all aspects of what the college does, thus stultifying the research process. It makes the more sensitive staff members uncomfortable about their participation in the enterprise. It turns questioners into antagonists and critics into false villains who can be accused of enmity toward the institutions.

### Lateral Versus Linear Data

> Our open-access mission demands that we provide as many services as possible to as many people as we can. There is no way for us to determine everything that our students gain by attending. The most important values may appear many years later. Besides, our college has multiple missions, and if we assess the effectiveness of any one of them, we devalue the others.

Community college leaders hold access as the highest purpose of the institution. The concept of the open-access college rests on student entrance. Enrollment data are monitored routinely because college funding depends on them. The percentage of a college district's population that attends the institution may be assessed periodically and steps taken to increase it. Growing enrollments are seen as an institutional good. State-mandated limitations on enrollment are anathema. Questions of what the students gain or where they go when they leave pale in the light of the attention that is paid to enrollment figures.

The problem of the missing data on student flow through the colleges relates also to different definitions of what constitutes education. Education can be seen as the activity of presenting information or as the process of effecting learning. According to the first definition, the proper area of study is the classroom, and the college environment and what the instructor does are the focus. Student ratings of their instructors and student access and retention rates are the most important data.

People who subscribe to the definition of teaching as the process of effecting learning take a different view. To them, student progress is the focus. They want to know what changes in student knowledge, skills, and attitudes occurred in a class or program and how many students became literate, graduated, transferred, and obtained jobs. Activities are considered only as they can be shown to be related to outcomes.

These opposing definitions affect the conduct of community college studies. Education as an activity is the dominant definition. Accrediting agencies do not chastise colleges because their students have not learned. State agencies do not base college funding on measurements of outcome. Data comparing scores made by graduates of various professional programs on state-administered exams in professional fields may be shared among states. But except for such measures as the Florida College-Level Academic Skills Test, which tie student test scores to graduation or transfer possibilities, college outcomes are rarely assessed in the aggregate.

Nearly all broad-scale measures of institutional outcomes have been imposed by legislators, not initiated by professional educators. Educators say that they oppose such measures because the varied student population precludes single measures of attainment. Actually, educators rarely use such measures because of the alternative definitions of instruction. Yet they despair over the minimal influence they have over the lives of their clients and are fearful of unwarranted comparisons that might jeopardize institutional support.

From the perspective of college staff members, the student body has a lateral form. Thousands of students arrive, thousands leave; they are numbered in the aggregate. But each student lives linearly. Each enrolls and progresses more or less deliberately toward an individual goal. And curricula are organized linearly, with course sequence and program requirements. The college is an environment with a conglomerate population that can be counted by gender, age, and ethnicity and a curricular conduit that propels people toward careers or further learning.

The prevailing concepts focus on the conglomerate. Most of a college's reports describe the student population, carefully broken down by every discernible characteristic, and the variety of activities in which they are engaged. Few reports take a linear view of the students as individuals moving toward defined goals as measured by educational objectives.

In the preface to the paperbound edition of his classic work, Hutchins notes higher education's "all-consuming fear" of defining goals, its "refusal to formulate precise ends, because the consequences will be . . . a confrontation with the necessity of a total conversion of our cultural mystique" ([1936] 1979, p. xvi). The generation of information follows from shared concepts. The nagging problem, the unresolved dilemma, is that the colleges' values are so set on lateral data that the linear data are ignored.

An effort by the U.S. Department of Education to reduce the student-loan default rate of $2 billion a year led to the recommendation that all colleges provide data on the graduation and job-placement rates of each of their programs. This recommendation received the predictable response accorded to initiatives emanating from extramural agencies: "community-college officials . . . oppose the requirement that they disclose graduation rates and job-placement records. The officials argue that doing so promotes misleading information and creates administrative burdens for colleges" (DeLoughry, 1990, p. A24).

## The Search for Reliable Data

Can the freeze on student-flow data be thawed? Information on college outcomes will be compiled only if college leaders ascribe as much importance to it as they do to the data on enrollments. If they collected information on student flow routinely, they would take extramural requests for data in stride. They need to convert their fear of knowing into an understanding of how the information can benefit the image, status, and ethical dimensions of their college.

The mission of the community college is manifold. Access is but one dimension of it. Other dimensions are learning, transfer, employment, and career advancement by students and an assortment of disparate educational and social objectives that fall under the heading of personal interest. All these educative and allocative goals suggest student movement or change. The students knew *this* when they entered, *that* when they left. They started at the college and *moved* on to a university. They *obtained* a new job or *advanced* on a career ladder. These concepts are longitudinal, not lateral. They suggest effects of a college going far beyond those that can be discerned from perusing enrollment figures, regardless of how those data are manipulated.

Numerous efforts have been made to turn the attention of college leaders to these effects. For years, the American College Testing Program has hosted conferences, convened committees, sponsored projects, and published reports that have furthered different forms of assessment. Various professional associations have encouraged their local affiliates to collect data on student entry into practice. Much of the legislation authorizing funds for occupational programs mandates the reporting of information on job entry.

Recently, the League for Innovation in the Community College has entered the lists by publishing a monograph on assessing institutional effectiveness (Doucette and Hughes, 1990). It describes the five major missions of colleges and offers questions that should be asked and the data sources by which they may be answered. It gives thirteen questions and data sources for the assessment of transfer, seventeen for career preparation, eleven for basic skills, fifteen for continuing education and community service, and thirteen for access. Those colleges that follow the suggested definitions for assessing effectiveness in even a few of the sixty-nine prescribed areas will move toward building the capacity to control their own flow of information.

Other initiatives have been put forward in the states. Florida's College-Level Academic Skills Test, New Jersey's Basic Skills Test, Texas's Academic Skills Program, and similar tests have been mandated for students seeking college entry, graduation, or transfer. The community college offices in some states publish compilations showing the number of graduates, transfers, and job entrants, in addition to the usual data on enrollments arrayed by gender, age, ethnicity, and county of residence.

Individual colleges occasionally report student-flow data, often in the course of evaluating their programs. A search of Educational Resources Information Center (ERIC) documents and the journal literature for the period January 1983 to June 1990 revealed 359 titles catalogued under community college program evaluation or program effectiveness. Of these, 67 assessed remedial and developmental programs; 98 covered vocational, technical, or job-training education; 40 were on general education or the liberal arts; and 27 were on continuing education or community service. (The remainder related to noneducative programs.) In addition, there were 204 follow-up studies: 56 related to career programs, 85 that surveyed graduates, and 23 related to students who transferred.

Various indicators can be generated if valid definitions are accepted.

- A *transfer rate* can be calculated by counting the number of students who enter in a given term with no prior college experience and who receive a minimum of twelve units at the college and matriculate at a university within the next four years.
- A *job-entry rate* can be defined as the number of students who enter a program related to an occupation with no prior experience working in that field and who within two years after leaving or completing the program obtain a position in the field.
- A *career-upgrading rate* can be defined as the number of students who enter a program related to an occupation after already working in the field for which that program is preparing people and who within two years advance in that same career.
- A *literacy rate* can be calculated based on the number of students who meet two definitions of literacy: learning to read and write better according to standard measures such as a reading or writing test and qualifying to enter college-level courses on completion of a pattern of remedial courses.

- *Gains in general education* can be calculated by administering subject area tests and student behavior inventories to sample groups of students, such as those enrolled in every Nth class section that meets on Wednesday at 10:00 A.M. or 7:00 P.M.
- *Personal interest achievement* can be estimated by asking random samples of students if they received from the college what they came for.

These indicators are valid measures of institutional mission and of student goals. They can be established and monitored routinely; a college can calculate perhaps one or two of them each year on a recurrent cycle. The colleges themselves control the process. No elaborate research enterprise is necessary. Information can be reported in a straightforward, readily understandable fashion, as in the following example.

Half the students who entered our college in 1985 with no prior college experience have completed four or more courses here. Of those, 25 percent have transferred to a university. We expect this rate to increase in the next few years as an effect of the strong agreements we have developed with our major receiving university.

Eighty percent of the students who enter with no prior experience in the field and who complete one of our health or technology programs obtain positions in that field within two years, but so do 75 percent of those who leave without finishing the program. Therefore, we need to examine our admissions and graduation requirements for the programs.

In the aggregate, half of the entrants who had been working in the area for which our occupational programs prepare people advance in that career within two years. The other half either stay in their job category or leave the field. We will compare these rates among our programs to see if there are differences.

Seventy percent of the students who completed at least forty hours of instruction in one of our literacy-development programs showed a gain of at least two grades in reading level and entered a college-level program, where we are monitoring their progress.

Our students learn what our courses purport to teach them. The gains in specified subject knowledge on a test of general academic ability average 12 percent for students who have taken one course in the subject area. This ranges from a 4 percent gain in our English classes to a 19 percent gain in the science classes.

A survey of a random sample of 10 percent of all the students who matriculated one year ago yielded an 82 percent response. Of those, 85 percent said that they had attained the goals they had set for themselves when they enrolled. The three goals most frequently noted were to gain job-entry skills, to learn skills useful in daily life, and to gain credits that could be used toward baccalaureate degrees.

The full studies on which these indicators are based are available on request.

A few college leaders and extramural agents have tried to establish such indicators. For example, the Center for the Study of Community Colleges at the University of California, Los Angeles, has pursued the issue by inviting a nationwide sample of community colleges to join a "transfer assembly" at no cost to the colleges (Cohen, 1990). The participating colleges provide data on the number of their students who enter in a given year with no prior college experience, complete at least twelve units at the college, and transfer within four years. Forty-seven colleges supplied the information on their 1984 entrants and more than 100 participated in the second round.

The colleges provided the data on student entrance and course-credit attainment and received the transfer information from their local universities or their state agencies, sometimes with center staff assistance. The transfer assembly encourages the colleges to build the capacity to generate their own information on student flow by insisting on a uniform definition of the transfer rate that is valid and readily understandable and for which the data may be feasibly acquired. But well over half the presidents who were invited to participate refused to take part on the grounds that the definition did not cover all contingencies, the data could not be retrieved, or the release of such information was perilous.

## Conclusion

The college leaders who generate information about institutional effects do much to mitigate unwarranted extramural criticism as they make the worth of their college self-evident and build a uniform data base to answer queries. But the real benefit of this process is that continued attention to outcomes shifts the staff members' view of their purpose by altering patterns of communication within and around the colleges. This shift in communicentricity takes the colleges away from the code of clandestine knowledge that they adopted from the universities, a code that has never suited community colleges.

The few genuine studies of program effects that appear each year suggest that the colleges have far to go before the gathering of information on institutional outcomes is routine. But the participation of colleges in well-designed projects shows their interest in defining these types of indicators. If this tendency spreads, it will do so from within because the influences that lead to an ethical code cannot come from outside the colleges. Data gathered grudgingly to satisfy an external agency are of little use in bringing about changes in staff members' perceptions. The data that people collect of their own volition are the only true reflection of their own values.

As a U.S. invention, the community college exhibits the quintessential characteristics of our culture: open access for self-elevation, forgiveness for past failings, the possibility of advancement regardless of family background, and the Horatio Alger notion of people being able to better themselves if only they try. These beliefs and values guide institutional practice. One more, a concern for outcomes, will add notably to the institution's rules of ethical behavior when it becomes central to the staff members' concerns.

In itself, not knowing outcomes is not unethical, but refusing to find them out is. Self-delusion is not unethical, but deliberate obfuscation is. The many purposes of the community college leave these institutions vulnerable to opportunistic behavior. But this vulnerability is not an excuse for avoiding knowledge of institutional effects. It is time to stop playing the shell game of "We don't provide data on transfer (or employment or general education and so on) because that would diminish our other missions." Community colleges will take a giant stride toward institutional ethics when they begin routinely assessing and reporting what happens to their students in each of their functional areas.

## References

Bender, L. W. "It Pays to Advertise—Truthfully." *Community College Review*, 1975, *3*(2), 32-39.

Boorstin, D. J. *The Image: A Guide to Pseudo-Events in America.* New York: HarperCollins, 1964.

Brint, S., and Karabel, J. *The Diverted Dream: Community Colleges and the Promise of Educational Opportunity in America, 1900-1985.* New York: Oxford University Press, 1989.

Cohen, A. M. "The Transfer Indicator." Paper presented at the annual convention of the American Association of Community and Junior Colleges, Seattle, Apr. 24, 1990.

DeLoughry, T. J. "Efforts by Cavazos to Curb Loan Defaults Draw Mixed Reaction." *Chronicle of Higher Education,* 1990, *36*(40), 1, A24-A25.

Doucette, D., and Hughes, B. *Assessing Institutional Effectiveness in Community Colleges.* Laguna Hills, Calif.: League for Innovation in the Community College, 1990.

Gordon, E. W., Miller, F., and Rollock, D. "Coping with Communicentric Bias in Knowledge Production in the Social Sciences." *Educational Researcher,* 1990, *19*(3), 14-19.

Hutchins, R. M. *The Higher Learning in America.* Westport, Conn.: Greenwood Press, 1979. (Originally published 1936.)

Karabel, J. "Community Colleges and Social Stratification." *Harvard Educational Review,* 1972, *41*, 521-562.

Karabel, J. "Community Colleges and Social Stratification in the 1980s." In L. S. Zwerling (ed.), *The Community College and Its Critics.* New Directions for Community Colleges, no. 54. San Francisco: Jossey-Bass, 1986.

Littlefield, W. P. "The Economic Impact of the Long Beach Community College District, Fiscal 1981." Long Beach City, Calif.: Long Beach City College, 1982. (ED 227 919)

London, H. B. *The Culture of a Community College.* New York: Praeger, 1978.

Moore, R. "Save Undergrads from the Maw of UC." *Los Angeles Times,* Aug. 15, 1991 (editorial).

Orfield, G. *The Chicago Study of Access and Choice in Higher Education: A Report to the Illinois Senate Committee on Higher*

*Education.* Chicago: Illinois Committee on Public Policy Studies, University of Chicago, 1984. (ED 248 929)

Pincus, F. L. "Vocational Education: More False Promises." In L. S. Zwerling (ed.), *The Community College and Its Critics.* New Directions for Community Colleges, no. 54. San Francisco: Jossey-Bass, 1986.

Richardson, R. C., Jr., Fisk, E. C., and Okun, M. A. *Literacy in the Open-Access College.* San Francisco: Jossey-Bass, 1983.

"Transfers Succeed at U of California." *Community, Technical and Junior College Times,* Aug. 1, 1989, p. 1.

Weis, L. *Between Two Worlds: Black Students in an Urban Community College.* New York: Routledge & Kegan Paul, 1985.

Wilcox, S. A. *Directory of Southern California Community College Researchers.* Los Angeles: Southern California Community College Institutional Research Association, 1987. (ED 287 529)

Zwerling, L. S. *Second Best: The Crisis of the Community College.* New York: McGraw-Hill, 1976.

# Chapter Three

# The President
# as Moral Leader

## Daniel F. Moriarty

If community college presidents are tempted to question the critical importance the public attaches to moral leadership, they need only recall the popular idols shattered by the public's outrage at misplaced trust. From Watergate in the 1970s to the Iran-Contra affair in the 1980s; from Bhopal, India, to Wall Street, New York; from the Congress of the United States to the boardrooms of savings and loan institutions, the stage is littered with once powerful leaders who have betrayed the public trust and wrought havoc on political, economic, and corporate identities. Far from the nation's public eye, less well known examples of moral failure have compromised university research, school boards, and college presidential leadership. In all cases, the public's outrage has been immediate, and the offender has had almost no chance for remorse and forgiveness. Despite the seeming broad tolerance, even fickleness, of the public in moral matters, betrayal of the public trust is invariably loudly condemned.

At the heart of the public's insistence on accountability lies an assumption that leaders must not violate the basic covenant that constitutes leader-follower relationships. This expectation clearly

51

extends to educational leaders. What might be tolerated in the corporate area will not be tolerated in the public arena and especially not in conduct related to education. In an opinion piece in the *New York Times,* William Simon, former secretary of the treasury, challenged President James Friedman of Dartmouth on the grounds of moral leadership and aptly stated the public expectation. He said, "The leaders of our colleges and universities, including Dartmouth, bear a high responsibility to their students and to society. . . . An explosive controversy at Dartmouth raises troubling questions about how its academic leadership is discharging its moral commitments and obligations to the college's students and to society" ("Demagoguery at Dartmouth," 1990, p. 25). Appropriately, Simon's attack was occasioned by Friedman's forceful moral denunciation of bigotry in the Dartmouth student newspaper. Despite the controversial nature of the particular incident, the battle is joined on moral grounds and assumes as a starting point the moral leadership of the president.

As community colleges enter this last decade of the twentieth century and assume an increasingly important role in educating our citizens for the next century, the role of the community college president in providing moral leadership will also become increasingly critical. The public will view community colleges as essential resources for workforce training, access to higher education, literacy improvement, and community development. Community college presidents will be asked to respond to these challenges at a time when resources are more limited than ever before, needs are more varied, and the public interests are fragmented.

Although presidents will be expected to have a rich repertoire of competencies, above all they will need to possess a moral compass and a vision that will guide their actions and decisions and that they can translate into leadership that best serves the individual and common good. As community college presidents examine their responsibility for moral leadership, they need to recognize that both philosophers and management scientists support the essential moral dimension of leadership, that opportunities for moral leadership in the community college abound, and that a clear and forceful statement of ethical responsibility can support and strengthen their role of moral leadership.

## The Ethical Dimensions of Leadership

At any level and in any sector in society, a public leader automatically takes on the responsibility of moral or ethical leadership. Gardner (1987), Burns (1978), and Badaracco and Ellsworth (1989) all argue that a leader must be judged in a framework of values and is an expert in the advocacy of values and that, preeminently, a leader's responsibility is moral leadership. Cox (1989) suggests the underlying reason why moral leadership is an essential and primary responsibility of the chief executive. Cox says, "When executives behold the corporation as the social institution—an interpersonal network committed to some mission in the service of customers, employees, shareholders and the public—it is not surprising that they think the management of values may be the ultimate description of their jobs" (p. 3).

The roots of this moral expectation can be traced to the reason that people join together in any society and what it is that keeps them together. Aristotle argued that people come together in society to achieve goals that they cannot achieve by themselves (Barker, 1959). These goals involve personal fulfillment, and personal fulfillment has everything to do with right human conduct, or that conduct most conducive to human happiness.

Philosophers have written extensively and disagreed significantly on the basic principles and underlying values of human conduct. They do agree that right human conduct is critical to individual fulfillment and that this conduct is subject to principles of behavior and to the values that underlie these principles. It is for these reasons that Aristotle saw the leader of a society primarily as a moral leader and saw ethics as a subset of politics (Barker, 1959). While writers of management science may not be students of Aristotle, they do recognize that organizations of people hold together and prosper because of the acceptance of basic values and principles of acceptable behavior. If the leader is not concerned about basic values and acceptable behavior, nothing else is possible.

Within the community college, the possibility of moral leadership rests on the assumption that morality, or right human conduct, is not subjective and variable but is based solidly on a core set of values that people can agree on. Gardner rejects any cynicism about the possibility of establishing a core set of values and calls for leaders who will espouse and defend traditional values based on freedom and justice, equality of opportunity, and the dignity and worth of the individual (Gardner, 1987).

Other, more specific, values derive from these core values, including tolerance, mutual respect, caring for others, integrity, individual empowerment, and individual moral responsibility. Bird and Waters (1989) talk about honest communication, fair treatment and competition, and safety as values. Bok's book *Lying* (1978) is a forceful and persuasively analytical argument on behalf of truth telling as a key value that binds together society at all levels. In his work on leadership, Burns (1978) stresses the importance of promise keeping as a key value, especially when he describes the responsibilities of political leaders.

Some of the very best arguments for the possibility of moral leadership are, of course, the examples of leaders in our own century who appealed successfully to the noble sentiments of large numbers of people and achieved outstanding results. In India, Gandhi helped his people overcome the country's factionalism and subservience to Great Britain and made them believers in a new, independent, and self-reliant Indian nation. On another continent, Martin Luther King, Jr., following Gandhi's powerful principle of nonviolence, awakened an entire nation to the menace of racism and to a dream of the worth and dignity of all people. At the outset of World War II, Churchill buoyed the courage of a beleaguered Britain in the face of Hitler's overwhelming war machine. More recently, Betty Friedan, through her writing and actions, brought about recognition of gender discrimination and inspired a renewed sense of identity and self-worth in women.

Burns (1978) sees leadership of this kind as moral and as transforming both the followers and the leader. "Transforming leadership ultimately becomes moral in that it raises the level of human conduct and ethical aspirations of both leader and led, and thus it has a transforming effect on both" (p. 20). In the dynamic of moral leadership, the leader and the followers reach new heights of achievement and aspiration and recognize their interdependency.

The powerful examples of the giants and near giants of political, national, and social leadership should not diminish the significance of moral leadership that takes place on lesser stages and in more obscure venues. At all levels, moral leadership is the responsibility of every leader who desires to move beyond the mere management of tasks, schedules, and processes to the leadership and elevation of people. The goals of moral leadership are all related to people, not to things. Gardner (1987), for example, says that a leader should believe in people; be concerned with the release of human potential; build community; share leadership; and lead others to accept responsibility, to exercise initiative, and to lead. Goals of this type are moral goals and constitute the elements of moral leadership. "But what separates a leader from a competent professional manager is the ability to build an organization that is a source of self-fulfillment and personal integrity for its members" (Badaracco and Ellsworth, 1989, p. 96).

### Responsibility for Moral Leadership

At the heart of the community college president's responsibility for moral leadership in interactions with others is the personal obligation of moral integrity. A leader's words and actions about moral leadership ring hollow when there is little evidence of the leader's personal integrity or personal awareness of ethics. This obligation does not suggest that leaders must follow a narrow, conforming pattern of behavior but does require of them personal beliefs and actions that resonate, mirror, and reinforce the espoused goals of moral leadership. The college president who is abusive and intolerant of the executive staff can hardly create a climate of teamwork and mutual respect. Nor can a president whose own attitude toward people of other races is negative develop an environment of equality of opportunity. A president who devises ingenious ways to keep decisions from undergoing public scrutiny undermines his or her credibility with staff and board members. Stakeholders always ask that the president's actions support the president's rhetoric.

Although many presidents do exemplify the passion and conviction of bona fide moral leaders, other educational leaders are reluctant to explicitly accept the mantle of moral leadership or even to engage in moral discourse. They may be reluctant to do so because many leaders feel awkward discussing a subject that seems to have been expropriated by a political-religious faction and has become identified with a rigid, conformist, right-wrong mentality. Leaders also may not wish to expose their lack of practice in moral discourse and their discomfort with the language and logic of ethical analysis. Educational leaders and the educational literature have not seen fit to discuss the ethical dimension of leadership, choosing instead to discuss the safer ground of organizational change, innovation, and achievement.

Several provocative explanations have been offered for the reluctance of leaders to embrace ethics as a key dimension of leadership. Bird and Waters (1989) suggest three explanations. They believe that leaders see talk about morals as a threat to harmony that requires personal confrontation, a threat to efficiency that obstructs responsible problem solving, and a threat to the image of power because it appears too idealistic.

Group-think within a community college can be as onerous as in business or industry. If harmony is a dominant value at a college, why would a president confront a sexist board member or an opportunistic legislator or admit to and expose institutional deficiencies? All these actions would surely disrupt harmony and may even put the president's tenure at risk. Skewed perceptions of team play can also lead to an abrogation of personal responsibility. When presidents suggest that staff members should "handle problems," they should be aware that they might be condoning any means to that end.

Whatever the etiology of the apparent reluctance to address the moral dimension of leadership in action or in discourse, the effects of this denial are not insignificant. Presidents can purposely limit their leadership role or see moral leadership as something nonessential and not highly valued. Faculty members expect, for example, that presidents will jump to the defense of academic freedom when self-appointed watchdog groups attempt to challenge a performance, a speaker, or the content of a course. The president who chooses to temporize on such a matter loses respect or even receives a vote of no confidence from the faculty.

Moral "amnesia" on the part of the system, Bird and Waters

(1989) note, can lead to a denial of abuses when they are all too apparent and unhealthy stress as the president attempts to deal with situations whose essential moral content is routinely ignored or denied. The unwillingness to recognize the moral implications of an issue or a decision can leave the community college president exposed and subject to serious if not devastating criticism. For example, to withhold important information from a board member is not just a matter of poor communication. If done intentionally, it may represent a serious abridgement of the president's obligation to tell the truth to those who have the right to the truth.

The president's relationship with board members is one area of significant moral obligation and potential conflict that could lead very quickly to a loss of moral authority and moral leadership. This fundamental relationship sets the moral tone for the entire institution. Fairness, truth telling, and respect for individual worth and dignity are some of the values that permeate the very close, personal, and at times confidential relationship between the president and the individual board members. In perhaps no other relationship is the nerve center of personal integrity and personal credibility so close to the surface. Presidents cannot be content to run the college and neglect the board, if neglect means not developing and nourishing through right conduct a relationship of trust, credibility, and mutual respect. Such a relationship is critical, and its quality or lack thereof properly justifies the continuation or noncontinuation of a board-president employment contract.

Boards have every right to demand ethical conduct of their presidents, based on established principles and expectations. Presidents must also demand the same from the board members. Community college presidents can take the initiative to shape their relationships with board members by actively and systematically promoting standards of fairness, full disclosure, honesty, and respect, both of themselves and of the board members. Presidential leadership can contribute significantly to empowering board members to reach their potential and to join fully in partnership with the president.

Presidential credibility is particularly tested by a variety of issues related to the curriculum, student success, and academic quality. Too many presidents of community colleges are perceived as "body counters" who are more concerned about state reimbursement than the quality of academic programs. This is not an image easy to change when funding mechanisms have historically been based on the number of students enrolled. Presidents of community colleges have risen to new heights, however, along with their institutions, when they have taken a firm stand on academic standards even at the risk of lost enrollments, revenue, and staff. In these instances, presidents have rightly chosen to embrace and reward values related to individual empowerment and accountability, high expectations, and courage. Their actions constitute moral leadership and have the potential of transforming themselves, the staff members, and the students.

Outside the college walls, presidents can also be tested in their relationships with corporations and organizations that seek educational services. Although colleges have an obligation to provide these services, presidents must ask themselves, At what point is the college up for sale and at what gain and for whom? One could argue that the student should be the chief beneficiary of the services and that the taxpayer should not be subsidizing the company. Neither should the president compromise the integrity of the college by (for example) violating or waiving college policies to accommodate special interests. The rush to be seen as industry's partner can easily lead presidents into promises they cannot keep or can keep only by actions that violate their trust with other stakeholders, for example, taxpayers or faculty members.

Clearly, the behavior that is most damaging to the president's personal integrity is that which is seen as accruing personal benefit to the president. College policy and state laws related to conflict of interest deter the more blatant and obvious violations but do not speak to the myriad situations of a more controversial and problematic nature. Relationships with professional associations, colleagues, universities, vendors, and sundry organizations, for example, require the president to decide whether the use of a college's resources is designed for the advantage of the college, the president, or both but mostly the president. Despite college leaders' best attempts at rationalization, not everything done or every dollar spent in the name of international education, professional development, or institutional advancement is done or spent for the sake of the institution.

Community college presidents need to assess carefully agreements with representatives of other countries that involve the sharing of resources and control, partially disclosed financial arrangements, and the extensive use of college time in travel and research, all under the flag and rhetoric of international education. Presidents might also subject decisions on staff development consultants and visiting speakers to an impartial process not unlike the request for a proposal process used to hire college architects or engineers, thus avoiding the perception that one hand is busy washing the other.

Presidents need to realize that these types of decisions are not entirely discretionary. Values and ethical principles may be at stake, and their violation, while relatively easy, may lead to a loss of integrity and an undermining of moral authority. Indeed, one could argue that the president, when in doubt about the ethical rightness of a decision, should always come down solidly on the side of right conduct. The president's credibility itself may be at stake. Why should the president ever run the risk of damaging that credibility? It is much better to run the risk of offending special interest groups or even popular wisdom than to sacrifice a key principle. Presidents who choose to think ethically will identify the problematic element in any issue and make a decision based on the solid ground of moral principle.

## Opportunities for Moral Leadership

Although opportunities for the undermining of moral leadership abound, magnificent opportunities for positive moral leadership on our college campuses also exist today. The following two situations, which took place only days apart, do not involve world-shaking events, but they illustrate the ethical problems that community college presidents face almost daily. They are significant because they involved good, decent people and recognized community college leaders. The examples also illustrate the opportunities available for moral leadership that exist as one labors in the presidential trenches. They show why the president must be concerned with ethical values and why the campus climate and culture must enhance ethical decision making rather than endorse plagiarism and situational ethics.

## Case One

Recently, it was discovered that a community college had taken eleven pages from a grant proposal of another college and had inserted it almost word-for-word into its own grant proposal. The proposals were to be judged on a competitive basis. No acknowledgment whatsoever had been given for the borrowed material—no quotation marks, no footnotes, nothing. When confronted with their action, several staff members within the institution that had done the borrowing responded that using the material was plagiarism only according to the artificial and subjective standards of others.

## Case Two

A president, when asked for advice by a community college professional on dealing with an employee who had falsified an employment application, said that the response should depend on whether the person was a team player. The president said that every effort should be made to protect the employee if the person was a team player. But, the president said, if the person was not a team player the incident was a good pretext on which to eliminate the person from the organization. At no time did the president express any concern for fairness, equality of treatment, or the seriousness of the offense. Needless to say, the questioner did not follow this advice. The president's response, of course, would never be forgotten, nor would the implications of leadership void of ethical considerations.

Diversity is an important issue on most college campuses today. However, a president whose interest in diversity begins and ends with avoiding litigation, keeping interest groups quiet, and achieving defensible ratios of diversity within the student body and staff is clearly not interested in moral leadership. While every president must achieve at least minimum goals related to diversity, moral leaders will seek to engage the entire college community in the values that underlie diversity and will reward actions based on these values. For example, the president can give resources and time to those divisions that participate in a staff development program aimed at intercultural understanding. Equality, respect for the dignity and worth of the individual, and justice are values that can potentially move a college community beyond inertia to a climate of rich cultural diversity that is manifested in curricula, activities, hiring and recruitment practices, civility on campus, and an abhorrence of bigotry. Specific goals, timetables, and resources need to be established in each area to achieve the desired effects.

The moral tone for this kind of campus climate can be most affected by the president. If the president does not create a vision of this ideal and establish high expectations, the mantle of leadership shifts or is dropped, and the campus moral climate deteriorates. If the climate for diversity deteriorates on a campus, invariably, the president will be held responsible. Presidents may say the fault lies in society, but people will respond that for this time and place, it rests with the president.

Another important opportunity for leadership revolves around individual empowerment and the acceptance of individual responsibility and initiative. In warning against the dream of mighty leaders who make the whole world right and absolve us of responsibility, Gardner (1987) calls for institutions and a society in which people are empowered to assume leadership, responsibility is shared, and organizations come alive because of the efforts of all stakeholders. Implicitly, Gardner speaks to the historical denial or avoidance of responsibility by individuals and groups in critical situations. Gardner says, basically, that such denial is immoral and unacceptable. Presidents who empower constituents, share leadership responsibilities, and insist on individual initiative and responsibility are leaders who believe in human possibilities and the power of people to renew themselves and their societies. "In the conventional mode, people want to know whether the followers believe in the leader; a more searching question is whether the leader believes in the followers" (Gardner, 1987, p. 11).

Presidents who see themselves as burdened with the responsibility of being the sole harbinger of a new vision have missed the central and pervasive value of shared leadership and also the opportunity to transform themselves and others through leadership. Some literature on college presidents exalts individual leaders and seems to absolve others of the responsibility for leadership or makes leadership appear to be a mysterious and magical art form. Inherent in this kind of thinking is the notion that the president conceives a vision of the institution and then works on others to inculcate that vision and to force the adoption of a company culture. Presidents who accept this role can do violence to individual liberty and to individual initiative. In such an environment, dissent would have no place, and a superficial solidarity—group-think—would masquerade as moral consensus. Most important, the worth and potential of the individual would not have been tapped for the benefit of all.

By building on a belief in the potential of every individual and enabling individuals to lead in turn, the president can liberate constructive and creative energy for the benefit of the individuals, the group, and the institution. This type of leadership is based on a belief in people's capacity to renew and rebuild their society. Communication by the president that discounts individuals or groups of employees runs counter to such a vision, becomes known, and gives the lie to contrary rhetoric.

Along with this faith in people comes the expectation that individuals will take responsibility and be recognized for their actions and for the quality of life around them. The type of confrontation this expectation requires is not always comfortable for the president or the constituents. Yet to empower people is to require them to be responsible for their use of power and to recognize their efficacy.

Presidents need to initiate discussion among the faculty and staff members about their responsibilities to each other, to the students, and to the community. Faculty members, for example, can play a significant role in setting standards and establishing the academic climate, but they are also responsible for the quality of teaching in their classrooms and for the climate of civility outside their classrooms. And at the same time that the president expresses concern for the quality of work life among staff members, he or she should also insist that they demonstrate care for individual students. In short, everyone on campus needs to assume personal responsibility for standards and excellence. The president exercises moral leadership by requiring individuals to accept this challenge and by recognizing those who do.

Perhaps the greatest opportunity for moral leadership by presidents lies in the challenge set forth by the Commission on the Future of Community Colleges in its publication *Building Communities*. The mission envisioned by this report focuses on the role of the community college in the development of community within the college and outside of it. The commission proposes that "the theme 'Building Communities' become the new rallying point for the community college in America. We define the term 'community' not only as a region to be served, but also as a climate to be created" (Commission on the Future of Community Colleges, 1988, p. 7).

The report envisions the classroom, the college, and the larger community all as arenas for community development. Basic to this vision is the conviction that our society is excessively fragmented and increasingly divided. Within our educational institutions, fragmentation and division occur between learners; learners and teachers; staff, faculty, and administration; and stakeholders in general. Race, money, education, power, and jobs all serve to divide. What can unite us are values—a common core of values that encourage diversity, differences, and dissent but that ultimately bind us all together.

Communities are important because they lead individuals beyond themselves to higher levels of accomplishment and aspiration. Communities strengthen, support, and teach individuals in relationship to each other and to the whole. Forming a community of learners, a community of educators, and a community of citizens constitutes an essential goal, however idealistic, of moral leadership. Without an appeal to permanent, underlying values that inform our relationships, however, this goal cannot be achieved.

*Building Communities* describes the values that have the capacity to bind us together (Commission on the Future of Community Colleges, 1988). The report talks about "the dignity and power of individuals" (p. 6) and "a concern for the whole, for integration and collaboration, for openness and integrity, for inclusiveness and self-renewal" (p. 7). The report also talks about a commitment "to open and candid communication, and to excellence for all" (p. 7). As a last and eloquent word, the epilogue states, "The influence of the community college must grow outward from a core of integrity and confidence firmly rooted in humane goals that are currently lacking in too many of our societal institutions" (p. 49). Clearly, only these values have the power to transform our actions, teaching, and services and to build a strong community. In his comments on community, another author says, "It is impossible to foster a sense of ongoing community without involving moral images and normative expectations" (Bird and Waters, 1989, p. 83).

## A Code of Ethics for Community Colleges

Recently, the heightened importance attached to the moral dimensions of leadership and the high public expectations of leaders have led to a renewed interest in organizational value statements and codes of ethics for institutional leaders. Universities across the country have started institutes and courses in ethics. Codes of ethics, once the preserve of doctors and lawyers, have also received renewed attention as a way of setting forth the standards to which leaders hold themselves. In her work *Lying*, Bok (1978) argues that scholars must consider the development of a code of ethics. "Scholars in many fields have had no reason in the past to adopt a code of ethics. But some are now exerting so much influence on social choice and human welfare that they should be required to work out codes similar to those that have long existed in professions like medicine or law" (p. xvii).

As chief executives of their institutions, presidents of community colleges clearly exert as much influence as and often have much more impact on the public welfare than scholars do. Presidents have broad discretion in the management of multimillion-dollar budgets, employ large numbers of staff members, manage sometimes hundreds of programs, and sign contracts for a variety of services. It seems appropriate to ask, therefore, that presidents of community colleges also make a strong professional statement on the importance of ethical values and moral leadership through a code of ethics that would set forth standards for their own behavior.

In addition to Bok's straightforward argument that educators need to be candid about their moral principles, other reasons to consider a code of ethics for presidents exist. A code need not be a listing of petty regulations. It can be a grand design that expresses a dearly and passionately held core of values that represent the ideals of the profession. As such, a code can foster pride, establish professonal identity, and build community among presidents who daily face difficult issues, anxious stakeholders, and needy communities.

In ambiguous situations, a code can also serve as a guide and a foundation for ethical behavior, even if it will never give the exact answer. When presidents face, for example, political pressures for the awarding of contracts and jobs, whether from board members or their shadows in the community, principles of conduct related to objectivity, fairness, and the best interests of the institution might be more helpful than a simple assessment of the immediate political pay-off of acquiescence to the pressure. Not surprisingly, presidents around the country find themselves in highly fluid and highly ambiguous situations for which there may be no obvious correct response. Indeed, it is entirely possible that two presidents facing the same problem may each reach a different solution. A carefully crafted code can provide basic principles on which such decisions can be based. Presidents should not have to make their way in the dark of a totally relativistic, subjective world.

A code of ethics can also serve as a guide and incentive to those who interact with the president. For example, employment contracts between presidents and boards are now incorporating ethical principles to serve as a basis for the board member's expectations and the president's obligations. Ethical values publicized in a code can put all stakeholders on notice that their president stands for certain principles that should not be assailed and will not be compromised. In any discussion or controversy, these principles can be a reference and a meaningful guide for decision making.

However, a public statement of ethics also provides a convenient evaluation instrument to measure the effectiveness of the president. Presidents have questioned whether a code of ethics might give their various publics one more "weapon" to turn against them. This is a curious argument in that it tries to limit a president's scope of responsibility, as if somehow people would then hold the president forever blameless. Presidents are always being evaluated on the basis of their moral leadership and integrity; principles have just never been explicitly laid out.

The principles contained in a code should not be seen as specific rules or regulations whose violation can be simplistically determined. Ethical principles should clearly reflect values and obligations, but these principles must always be applied to specific situations in which responsible people can reasonably disagree.

Presidents need to accept once and for all their accountability, not only on technical grounds but also on moral grounds. Frankel (1989) makes this point in his article on codes. Frankel says that "because the profession affects the interests and well-being of individuals who depend on professional services and also exert influence on key social institutions that pursue the common good, society has every right to evaluate professional performance in the light of a moral as well as a technical dimension" (p. 110). If a code of ethics is well crafted, presidents should be eager to take a stand even if they are criticized for doing so.

Presidents of community colleges across the country have worked for the past two years through their national organization, the American Association of Community and Junior Colleges (AACJC), to develop a code of ethics specifically designed for community college presidents. The completed code includes a preamble, a statement of values, and a set of principles. In the preamble, the president's primary role as the moral leader of the institution is explicitly set forth. The preamble also includes a clear recognition of the limitation of the code and of its basic heuristic value.

The statement of values in the code describes the values that inform and underlie the principles of conduct. The values tend to cluster around the twin mandates of justice and liberty. All the values described—honesty, fairness, respect for individual people, and excellence, for example—constitute a shared core of values that must first be accepted if the principles of conduct are to be maintained.

The principles of ethical conduct in the code have to be understood as standards from which action flows. The principles are set forth as responsibilities toward the major stakeholders, including board members, faculty and staff members, students, and the larger community. The code is a call to action in relation to the constituent members of the community, not a plea for passive, private virtue involving being and not doing. The president must be a person of virtue, that is, possess a certain quality of character. But the code requires the president to do, act, urge others in the college community to assume their ethical responsibilities and acknowledge the contributions of others.

Despite the benefits inherent in a code of ethics for community college presidents, the limitation of such a code in promoting ethical behavior and ethical leadership is obvious. A code only describes standards of conduct; it does not by itself require or inspire ethical leadership. The life and force of the proposed code of ethics will be that given to it by community college presidents who are convinced of their ethical responsibilities. Obviously, presidents need to read and discuss the code. More important, presidents need to begin to think ethically and to engage in ethical discourse.

## Discussions of Ethics on Campus

One of the greatest benefits growing out of the recent national attention focused on the ethical dimensions of community college leadership is the beginning, in one state after another, of workshops and seminars on ethics specifically related to the responsibilities of the community college president. The need for discourse in ethics and for education in ethical thinking is clear. Moral issues and moral challenges are by definition difficult, perplexing, and impervious to simple solutions. For example, how many presidents in the throes of budgetary cutbacks have been cited by their constituents as unfair, unjust, uncaring, and injurious to the public good? The downsizing of a budget involves more than financial decisions, and presidents who must make these decisions might well profit from a collegewide discussion on the human impact of the budget cuts in terms of fairness, promise keeping, and openness. Holding such discussions may not be efficient and may make the president seem less than decisive, but the discussions constitute an ethical approach that could actually generate a better decision.

While ethical thinking and moral leadership assume fidelity to the laws of the land and the policies of the institution, they are most brought into play in complex situations where moral principles can serve only as a guide to action. In his article on moral reasoning in U.S. public administration, Chandler (1983) forcefully states the president's position: "Many administrators live in a no-man's land of what is lawful, what is wise, and what is in the public interest. The real question is not whether they inhabit the land of moral ambiguity, but how well equipped they are to survive in it without seeking refuge in bureau-pathology" (p. 37).

Drake and Baasten (1990) begin to describe a structure in which to frame ethical thinking. They list and describe five stages of moral argument: problem definition, stakeholder analysis, normative evaluation, decision making, and reflection. This structure makes clear that ethical thinking need not be some mysterious incantation or trance but can be translated to understandable, even prosaic, elements that can be learned and practiced by anyone—not unlike any other critical thought process.

Another important reason for discussion on moral values and moral responsibilities in our colleges is that without discussion there is little chance that a real concern for values and the ethical implications of our actions will take root and flourish. Dialogue about morality tends to raise the critical issues and encourages people to take specific positions related to these issues.

According to Baasten and Drake (1990), "Dialogue helps to test and clarify the values of both the leader and followers and encourages them to find more creative solutions to moral dilemmas that arise in the workplace" (p. 4). Presidents need to take the lead in raising moral issues and in insisting that the moral dimension of any issue be faced. They might, for example, initiate a dialogue on their campus about the role of part-time faculty members and their use and potential abuse. This issue is not simply a staffing question. Individual faculty members can be hurt, students can be cheated, and a program's quality can deteriorate—all in the name of an efficiency that ignores ethical concerns. An open discussion of the issue involving both full- and part-time faculty members might lead to a much better decision and one that is supported by more people than a decision made by a few and based entirely on economics.

Too often, in fact, decisions are made as if an issue were merely a question of organizational strategy, expediency, or public relations. It is only when the expediency of the moment is reported on the front page of the local newspaper that the moral dimension of the issue becomes unmistakably clear. In an institution where the president is known to raise moral issues, the ethical aspects of an issue will be addressed and others in the college community will readily join in identifying and discussing the moral dimension of decision making. The primary responsibility for initiating and rewarding moral discourse, however, remains with the president.

If moral discourse becomes a reality on college campuses and if presidents engage in public discussion of ethical questions, then a code of ethics may have some real meaning for presidents, their constituents, and their institutions. Organizations of state community college presidents and the AACJC can promote and support a new awareness of the pivotal importance of shared ethics to presidential leadership. This dimension of professional development for presidents should be a long-term effort, not a gesture occasioned by a currently popular topic. Professional associations need to protect and support their constituents. In seeing to the professional integrity and ethical literacy of their member presidents, professional organizations fulfill one of their most important responsibilities. They serve also to protect and support the profession and can propel members into a critical moral leadership role, a responsibility sadly neglected in most of the organizations in our society.

## Conclusion

The public's loss of confidence in its institutions and in its leaders does, in fact, present an opportunity for educational leaders across the country to sound a different theme. Regrettably, educational leaders are not always seen today as the moral leaders whom the public respects. Indeed, sometimes they are seen as part of the problem, even, as President Trachtenberg of George Washington University points out, symbolic of the deterioration of values in our society (Trachtenberg, 1989).

Public institutions and their presidents seem increasingly vulnerable to criticism by the public and by the press. Invariably, the harshest criticism is reserved for the perceived lack of moral leadership, whether for lack of personal integrity or for failure to seize the moral initiative and lead. Community colleges today demand, more than anything else, moral leadership. The public interest and welfare of the people are at stake, and the presidents of community colleges are the stewards of the public trust. The time to recognize the moral dimension of leadership is now. The time to seize the opportunity for moral leadership is also now. Community college presidents must think and behave as if ethics and moral leadership were their natural and most important responsibility.

## References

Baasten, M. J., and Drake, B. "Ethical Leadership." Paper presented at the annual conference of the National Social Science Association, Vancouver, Canada, Mar. 1990.

Badaracco, J. L., Jr., and Ellsworth, R. R. *Leadership and the Quest for Integrity*. Boston: Harvard Business School Press, 1989.

Barker, E. *The Political Thought of Plato and Aristotle*. Mineola, N.Y.: Dover, 1959.

Bird, B., and Waters, J. A. "The Moral Muteness of Managers." *California Management Review*, Fall 1989, pp. 73–87.

Bok, S. *Lying*. New York: Pantheon, 1978.

Burns, J. M. *Leadership*. New York: HarperCollins, 1978.

Chandler, R. C. "The Problem of Moral Reasoning in American Public Administration: The Case for a Code of Ethics." *Public Administration Review*, Jan.–Feb. 1983, pp. 32–39.

Commission on the Future of Community Colleges. *Building Communities: A Vision for a New Century*. Washington, D. C.: American Association of Community and Junior Colleges, 1988.

Cox, A. "Focus on Teamwork, Vision and Values." *New York Times,* Feb. 26, 1989, sec. 3, p. 3.

"Demagoguery at Dartmouth." *New York Times,* Oct. 20, 1990, p. 25.

Drake, B., and Baasten, M. "Facilitating Moral Dialogue and Debate: A New Leadership Dimension." Paper presented at the Western Academy of Management, Shizuoka Management Conference, Shizuoka, Japan, June 1990.

Frankel, M. S. "Professional Codes: Why, How, and with What Impact?" *Journal of Business Ethics*, 1989, *8*, 109–115.

Gardner, J. W. *The Moral Aspect of Leadership*. Leadership Papers, no. 5. Washington, D.C., INDEPENDENT SECTOR, 1987.

Trachtenberg, S. J. "Presidents Can Establish a Moral Tone on Campus." *Educational Record*, Spring 1989, pp. 4–9.

**Part Two**

# Shaping and Maintaining Ethical Policies and Practices

# Chapter Four

# Ethics in Instructional
# Programs

## Florence B. Brawer

Just a few years ago, the title of this chapter would have sounded ludicrous to most educators and even more ridiculous to most lay-persons. Most people would have thought it pointless to discuss, let alone question, ethics in the instructional program or in the class-room, whether at the elementary or graduate level. Good teachers were assumed to have exemplary behavior. Educational programs that were selected by the schools or state were thought to be justi-fiable and positive for all students. If problems occurred in the classroom, they were thought to be generated by the students them-selves, certainly not by the instructors.

Today, ethical concerns are so apparent and expressed so intensely in the political and social arenas, and we are becoming more willing to face the reality of what transpires in colleges and universities. We realize that the above viewpoints are both naive and abstract. Classrooms are not always seats of democracy, nor do they offer opportunities for educating all students. Problems cannot be blamed on the students alone; faculty members as well may have difficult personalities. Faculty members do not invariably conduct themselves in an ethical manner. All instructors are not effective in teaching students, that is, moving them to changed behavior and to the acquisition of particular knowledge and skill.

This chapter discusses some of the ethical issues surrounding academic programs. The section called "Ethics in the Curriculum" discusses computer use along with ethics in other curricula. "Ethics and the Faculty" discusses instructors as role models and members of a profession that, by definition, must have a code of ethics. It also relates authoritarianism to sexual harassment. "Ethics in the Classroom" extends concepts of ethics to student behavior. "Ethics and Administrative Issues" discusses guidelines for employing faculty members.

## Ethics in the Curriculum

Most professions have established codes of ethics. At the same time, "constant changes in societal values, market place demands, organizational operating procedures, and public standards of conduct, are making it increasingly difficult to delineate which behaviors are and are not acceptable" (Whisnant, 1988, p. 244). Because of their relative youth as compared to their four-year counterparts, community colleges do not have many traditions or past experiences to guide behavior. Further, the comprehensive mission of the colleges diffuses whatever resources are available.

The most significant ethical issues in community colleges do not develop from deeply thought-out philosophical problems but rather from stretched interpretations of policy. Making a noncredit flower arranging activity into a course providing college credit, for example, raises ethical issues and threatens the public reputation of a college. This example typifies the ethical problems that are faced by community college financial officers and administrators. A number of community colleges have suffered attacks on their integrity, their judgment, and even their role in higher education because they stretched policy to meet budgetary limits. Administrators often must decide if it is more important to gain dollars now or to build a good reputation in the future.

## Computer Courses

Weak ethical standards have led to an increase in computer-related crimes. To offset these crimes, educational institutions must teach students not only the use of computers but also the moral implications inherent in that use. Gottleber (1988) says that the increase in crimes involving computers and the characteristics of the average computer criminal point to the "academic role as one of the primary breeding grounds for this type of criminal" (p. 51). Students are taught sophisticated ways to gain access to and to manipulate computer data, but they are seldom taught about appropriate and inappropriate uses for computers.

Indeed, few community college curricula even touch on the topic of ethics as it relates to data processing. Curriculum planners seem to assume that whatever ethical standards students possess come from the home environment or other sources. In a survey of several colleges, Gottleber (1988) found that the best any community college did as far as teaching the moral underpinnings of data processing was the possible mention of ethical considerations in a lecture in an introductory computer science course. No institution that he contacted required students to take courses in the ethics of data processing, and few even had a course to recommend to those who were concerned with ethical behavior.

Several chairpersons of computer science departments expressed doubt as to the ability of any member of their staff to teach this type of course. Others explained that such a course did not even belong in the department but rather in the department of philosophy. However, despite concerns as to where and to whom this course ought to be delivered, they expressed a strong desire that they and their faculty members be informed about any research and developments in the area of ethics in data processing (Gottleber, 1988).

Most important, perhaps, is Gottleber's statement (1988) that if community college students can understand the position of trust that they have been given, the institutions can attempt to integrate the technology of the future and the ethical standards historically held to be important. Students need to explore not only the societal implications of criminal behavior but the personal ramifications as well. How can individuals feel good about themselves when they have been party to criminal actions? The criminality of certain actions with the computer and the result of computer-related crimes must be made clear to students.

All institutions involved in the dissemination of knowledge about computer use and data processing should try to help their students develop ethical standards regarding access to data. A course in ethics in data processing, which could apply to other areas of the curriculum as well, would include among its several purposes (1) exposing students to a number of situations that involve choices between ethical and unethical options, (2) exploring situations in which individuals have historically made unethical choices, (3) examining the costs of computer crime from both a business and societal perspective, (4) presenting the role of the computer professional in contemporary society, (5) placing students in real-life scenarios where they are forced to make ethical decisions, (6) studying society's reaction to computer-related crime, and (7) helping students realize that even though they have "an almost God-like power at their fingertips, the mundane rules of ethical behavior cannot be suspended" (Gottleber, 1988, p. 53).

Brunner (1988) notes that computer software is currently being copied and used illegally in school settings. He recommends that computer law courses be developed so that instructors can teach the legal requirements to their students. Hoiles (1989) argues for the evaluation of ethics in the total community college business curriculum. Newspaper headlines and other sources illustrate dishonest business practices and the need for a moral reorientation, which could be brought about in part by specially designed courses to teach business ethics, review of students' responses to questions about business ethics, and consideration of the development of a code of ethics.

### Other Curricula

All curricula and all programs should be periodically examined for their ethical dimensions. In accounting education, for example, ethics should be integrated into the program, an idea that dates back many years. Arguing that business programs in community colleges need to provide moral guidance and leadership to help stem the proliferation of fraudulent and questionable financial reporting practices, Clarke (1990) notes, "Whether it is ignorance or greed that beguiles business people into unethical behavior, the educational system must provide a moral foundation for its students. There is a school of thought which argues that students who are college age have already established their moral values, and so the discussion of ethics in the classroom will have no impact on ethical problems, and will not change students' moral values. While this argument is often advanced in opposition to the teaching of ethics, adult behavior should be influenced by universal moral principles, and these principles must be taught" (pp. 13-14).

Examples of ethical abuses, pressures to respond to reports, failure to disclose significant information, and changing accounting policies could all be integrated into courses. Monetary abuses in the defense industry alone suggest that cost accounting is a fertile area for including ethical issues in the curriculum.

A course for associate degree nursing students could similarly involve ethical concepts. Roediger (1984) addresses such issues as bioethics, ethical concepts, decision making, and legal perspectives on ethics in nursing practice. The Community College Humanities Association is also concerned with the teaching of professional ethics. Wright (1985) argues that collaboration between philosophy and technical instructors is important in developing and teaching professional ethics so that case studies may be examined from ethical and practical viewpoints.

Less equivocal than Wright's is the argument to include ethics instruction within the liberal arts. Edmonson (1989) traces the place of ethical and moral instruction in higher education from the nineteenth century, when moral philosophy was considered an integral part of the mission of a college, through the period when religious and ethical instruction were removed from the purview of research universities, to the current resurgence of interest in reinstating Western values into the curriculum. The conventional wisdom in the academic establishment that condemned ethics instruction and moral education is partly responsible for the decadence and decay of modern society, according to Edmonson. Instruction in ethics, religion, and democratic values should be liberal, and instruction in ethics should be included in the curriculum of every college in order to develop an educated and ethical workforce.

The difficulties inherent in integrating ethics with other subjects are observed by Laney (1990), who reports that the university or college "seems to have no way to address a major ethical issue that does not comport with its understanding of itself or its task [because it] . . . perceives itself as performing an educational function rather than engaging in a moral enterprise" (p. 51). The college is therefore left with no way to examine itself in relation to the common good.

Colleges may have been committed to truth in the most general sense from the beginning but this was "the truth that made one free." This truth was the education of young people for participation in the community, not for a direct confrontation with community values. The earliest colleges tried to help students form values and to channel their aspirations on behalf of the community, but it would not have occurred to any early college faculty or staff members to take a position on changing society directly. And even that much attention to the students' participation in the polity was lost when the academic disciplines broke up knowledge and when institutional ties between the colleges and the external entities of church and state were weakened. Now the college is living on the moral authority it accrued in its early years (A. M. Cohen, personal conversation, Sept. 29, 1991). The structures might look the same, but the moral dimension is absent.

### Civic Literacy

The loss of morality in our era may be compared with the loss of morality in earlier times, such as during the presidencies of Warren G. Harding and Ulysses Grant. Although some educators living early in this century—for instance, John Dewey, James B. Conant, and Robert M. Hutchins—explored various facets of the transference of values, the 1980s provided an example of a moral malaise in which individual avarice surpassed the regard for moral standards identified by the early twentieth-century leaders. Arguing for the development of "civic literacy" through education, Parsons (1989) suggests that there may be a positive response to the question

"Does America's higher education community consider the development of values, ethics, morals—the fostering of civic literacy—a legitimate role to be played?" (p. 6).

One approach to implementing civic literacy supports Parsons's thesis. Since 1979, when Hagerstown Junior College in Maryland conducted its first ethics colloquium, a number of faculty members, students, administrators, and community residents have analyzed such diverse topics as social change, leadership, and the new corporate system. Parsons maintains that if a college wishes to assist its community in developing civic literacy, the colloquium process is an effective way to do so because a "sense of commitment, participation, and direction will emerge" from the teaching of civic literacy (1989, p. 8). This approach, then, becomes a commitment to community interaction of a very high order.

Throughout the 1980s, educational writers implored colleges to select a curriculum that nurtures intellectual values as well as teaches about them. Values, ethics, and a moral point of view are considered essential to the quality of life, and colleges have been perceived as having potential civic functions that no other single institution can provide. The development of civic literacy is a legitimate role for America's higher education community. Colleges should forget their institutional egos, develop leadership devoted to preventing misconduct, and become involved in social needs and concerns, and students should be encouraged to express their concern with the consequences of unethical behavior (Parsons and Powell, 1988).

## Ethics and the Faculty

It is not uncommon for both the academic literature and the popular press to emphasize the importance of the teacher as role model. Students' reactions to these role models vary considerably. They may perceive instructors as being extremely authoritarian and may be blind to the trap that this characteristic can involve. Some students resist the identity of the instructor just because it is so attractive to them. Still others shop around for role models, adopting a teacher's mannerisms while still maintaining their own resources to incorporate the esteemed qualities.

Although only the grossest of generalizations can describe the 275,000 faculty members teaching in U.S. community colleges, it is possible to point out certain demographic features of this group. Fewer males teach in community colleges than in universities but more than in secondary schools. Most faculty members hold the master's degree or have had equivalent experiences in their particular occupational area. Around 25 percent of the academic-course instructors have a doctorate, fewer than in the university. The emphasis is on teaching rather than research or scholarly inquiry. Full-time instructors typically conduct four or five classes per term, thirteen to fifteen hours weekly. Salaries tend to be higher than in secondary schools but lower than in universities. Many full-time instructors, as well as the 60 percent of the instructors who work part time, have other jobs in addition to their teaching. The full-time instructors teach three-fourths of the classes (Cohen and Brawer, 1989).

With the exception of increases in age and teaching experience, faculty demographics have remained surprisingly consistent over the years. From the 1920s to the 1960s, community college instructors tended to have had prior secondary school teaching experience. As the number of newly employed instructors declined by the 1970s, however, the proportion of instructors with such previous experience also declined, since community college faculty came directly from graduate school and not from jobs in the secondary schools. In the 1970s, many graduate students declared their intentions to teach in community colleges early on, and university higher education programs expanded rapidly if they included a community college component.

### Faculty as Role Models

Early studies that attempted to assess good teaching and to identify the so-called good teacher equated good with "good girl or boy scouts." The feeling still prevails that teachers should act as positive role models for their students, that is, as mature individuals who will focus on the direction that the students are assumed to be taking. But what does the mature instructor look like? Cohen and Brawer (1972) describe such an instructor. "The person with a strong ego, a firm sense of self, is able to cope with and to integrate the intrinsic and extrinsic forces . . . can accept the bureaucracy, the petty regulations, and the imprecise goals of the organizations; the different students and the recurrent changes within . . . [the academic] field, and still maintain a clear, consistent sense of . . . direction. The ability to withstand what are sometimes extremely demanding forces that tend to conflict with one's internal value system suggests a high level of ego development" (p. 10).

Maturity—of a person, a profession, or an institution—is demonstrated by the desire to be judged on the basis of products and effects. For college instructors, maturity means integrating a consciousness about self with a sense of professionalism and purpose. Truly mature individuals are open to experiences and free to focus on their profession. They turn from a preoccupation with self to a concern for others.

No instructor functions in isolation, disassociated from students, colleagues, or the educational milieu. Teachers are tied to their own hierarchies of values and the attitudes stemming from these values. They are products of their personal and their collective experiences, but they also interact with students, colleagues, and the institutions with which they are affiliated. They may be true to themselves, autonomous, powerful, and certain of themselves and their directions, but the person who would function well cannot operate apart from either environmental or interpersonal forces. Thus teachers must be considered as unique and complex people who are tied to others in equally complex ways. Their classroom activities and the way they conduct themselves serve both as models to the students whom they attempt to teach and also as extensions of their individual selves. Whatever role models a teacher projects, the modeling of ethical conduct must be paramount because there should be no room in the classroom for unethical mannerisms or expressions.

In addition to acting as positive role models, faculty members must be involved in their teaching and in developing within their profession. In a paper entitled "The Faculty Member as Recluse," Cohen (1976) presented new terms for describing instructors who do not continue to seek professional growth. "I see them as isolates, as pariahs, as outcasts—from the academic discipline for which they were trained, from the universities and secondary schools, and from broad currents of two-year colleges, their host institutions. They are in an eddy, away from a main stream. And they have placed themselves there of their own volition" (p. 2).

Many of these so-called pariahs "hide behind the classroom door" (Cohen, 1976, p. 2). If they insist on closing these doors and hiding behind perquisites in their contracts so that no one knows the extent to which their students have learned, it is impossible to tell how effective they are. Until these faculty members emerge from their isolation, they will continue to be a reclusive group that prides itself on privacy, cuts itself away from academic affiliation, refuses to attempt to understand the discipline of instruction, ignores ideas stemming from outsiders, scorns administrators, shuns the community, abandons part-time instructors who teach the same courses, and treats with derision its own members who become managers of student learning rather than the single authority in the classroom. Those instructors who become isolated within their own institutions are both nonprofessional and unethical.

## Professionalism

The term *professionalism* suggests that the members of an occupational group (education, law, or medicine, for example) display elements of peer judgment or self-policing, perform on behalf of clients or audiences, incorporate a body of specialized knowledge that is not readily available to laypersons, adopt a communal sense of identity, endure long periods of training, and develop—and practice—a code of ethics. Professional groups must police themselves if they are to ensure ethical behavior among their members. However, faculty organizations in community colleges generally exhibit only a modest form of self-policing. They have successfully warded off most attempts by governing boards, legislators, and administrators to make judgments about who should be dismissed, but the ultimate power to employ and retain instructors still remains with the governing boards of the institutions. Faculty members, as members of a profession, have failed to develop succinct, reliable, and readily understood guidelines for peer review, and it is unlikely that they will do so. Evaluation procedures typically call for faculty review committees to consult with instructors under review and to make every effort to assist them in improving both within and outside the classroom according to vague standards of professionalism.

It is rare for a faculty committee to recommend that a faculty member be dismissed. Only instructors who blatantly exhibit untoward behavior—who fail to meet classes or display immoral behavior—are called to task. Professional groups tend to protect their members, and faculty groups should and generally do assist their members to attain high levels of professional practice.

Faculty groups must develop and distinctly spell out criteria for professional practice. They must establish criteria, set definitive goals, and follow appropriate evaluation procedures.

The single most important criterion for good teaching should be student achievement. Faculty members can exhibit ethical behavior in the classroom by stressing specific learning objectives and by seeing that students achieve the enunciated goals. This approach equates teaching with learning. It suggests that every student can learn and that the teacher has an ethical imperative to see that students are brought from one place on the learning spectrum to another.

Moonlighting among instructors also evokes the question of responsibility. While many instructors may be forced to moonlight by economic forces and others who do take dual positions may be accountable to both, some tend to let their teaching obligations slip. Is it ethical for instructors to assign little work or fewer papers because they have no time to read assignments? Is it ethical for any instructor, moonlighting or not, to skim over reports and disregard the students' work by not making appropriate comments?

The assessment of student learning, then, becomes both the ultimate criterion of good teaching and a measure of teaching accountability. The perception of student progress toward specific learning objectives must be seen as the definitive purpose of an institution. Nearly all institutions engage in some type of evaluation—from pro forma procedures to genuine attempts to positively affect instruction and assess instructional behaviors. All efforts to evaluate faculty members should be seen as direct ways of assessing accountability.

## Authoritarianism and Sexual Harassment

Psychologists and political scientists who in the 1930s and 1940s addressed themselves to the potential effects of extremist political movements on American ideology saw authoritarianism as a basic dimension of personality. This idea is well described in *The Authoritarian Personality* (Adorno, Frenkel-Brunswik, Levinson, and Sanford, 1950), in which the authors postulated nine components of the syndrome that were developed from Freudian concepts. This same idea of authoritarianism is directly related to the interaction of instructors with students and with their colleagues.

In 1960, Waller described the interaction between teachers and students as "a special form of dominance and subordination, a very unstable relationship in a quivering equilibrium, not much supported by sanction and a strong arm of authority, but depending largely upon purely personal ascendancy. Every teacher is a taskmaster, and every task-master is a hard man; if he is naturally kindly, he is hard from duty, but if he is naturally unkind, he is hard because he loves it" (p. 334).

Just as creative instructors may foster creativity among their students, authoritarian instructors have their own effects. They encourage either countervailing authoritarianism or subordination or complete disregard. When one person acts authoritatively and the other submits, either through choice or through fear, the subordinate person fragments his or her personality. Waller (1960) maintains that subordination is possible only because the subordinated person exhibits but a mere element of personality while the dominant one participates completely. Both authoritarianism and the resultant submissiveness on the part of the student are undesirable.

Sexual harassment is an extension of authoritarianism in the extreme, an example of a power relationship gone awry. In 1991, with the Clarence Thomas–Anita Hill confrontation regarding alleged sexual harassment, a problem that long had been surfacing came to a point of national consciousness. Although Thomas was eventually confirmed as a Supreme Court justice, the hearings left a certain taint as well as a new sensitivity among many people. The whole question of sexual harassment was brought into the forefront.

Of course, sexual harassment also occurs in business and academic settings. And to say that sexual harassment is a violation of ethics within or outside of the classroom is to make a point that seems redundant. However, if both instructors and students are aware of the negative implications and consequences of these acts, perhaps the situations will be altered and the existence of sexual harassment will be minimized.

Pointing out problems that appear on some campuses, Dziech and Weiner (1984) declare that "sexual harassment of college students by their professors is a fact of campus life that many educators learn to ignore and, in their silence, to accept. . . . The silence is part of the problem, ignoring the issue only makes it worse" (p. 1). While most charges of sexual harassment deal with women being harassed by men, there are incidences of female professors harassing male students or homosexuals harassing colleagues. Each problem exists in several forms, and each demands different types of analyses.

Sexual harassment on campus will be eliminated only when doing so is the concern and responsibility of all those who associate with the institution. If campus climates are to change, both men and women who work in colleges—students, deans and department heads, and administrators—must lead the way. "Because of recent media attention to sexual harassment, the legal liabilities of institutions and the increased litigiousness of students and employees, higher education must police itself. If it does not, it risks being policed by other institutions and forces with less sensitivity and understanding of the academic environment. Administrators responsible for making campus policy will need to consider steps involved in establishing prevention, grievances, and sanction procedures" (Dziech and Weiner, 1984, pp. 169–170).

As long as faculty members do not abuse their professional autonomy, as long as they use it legitimately in classrooms and laboratories as teachers and scholars, such autonomy is laudable, defendable, and essential to the academic endeavor. But autonomy can create problems. Instructors may develop an exaggerated sense of self-importance. They may feel like deities within the sanctuary of their classroom, laboratory and office; dictate attendance, study, and grading policies; and exercise absolute control over content, interpretation, and methodology of the course. Students are completely at the mercy of these instructors, and both parties know it. When sexual harassment occurs in this setting, the results can be devastating.

We should be able to increase our understanding of one person's word against another when seeking to verify charges of sexual harassment by systematically investigating and analyzing situations. Although fewer cases may lack corroborating evidence, more information may be needed to substantiate them. And since we as faculty members work in isolation, treating each situation as if it were unique, our "passion for privacy" often outweighs our common sense. Cooperative research projects on different campuses could discover commonalities in cases and foster discussion in professional organizations so that college leaders would be better prepared to judge future grievances (Dziech, 1991).

The effects of harassment on attitudes and performances are not limited to the victims. Cases of sexual harassment give rise to the question of morality among all members of the academic community. In the 1980s, almost every college campus adopted a policy or statement dealing with sexual harassment. According to Small (1990), colleges are ethically bound to "create an institutional framework in which sexually harassing behavior is defined, the institution's attitude toward such behavior is announced, a process for bringing complaints is created, and the range of sanctions is made clear" (p. 251).

Many gray areas exist in a definition of sexually harassing behavior. These include whether or not sexual harassment covers all kinds of misconduct that is gender related or is narrowly limited to behavior, covers generic slurs or is limited to obscene or suggestive remarks, includes speech or only physical conduct, involves a power imbalance between the parties or can occur between faculty colleagues or fellow students, and covers consenting behavior.

Clearly enunciated policies dealing with sexual harassment that are specified in advance and written according to general ethical principles are essential. By making such policies known, an institution identifies itself as a moral institution. Little (1989) reinforces this thesis by arguing that colleges can minimize unethical conduct by formally adopting a code of ethics or adding statements about appropriate sexual relationships to existing sexual harassment policies. Faculty senates on six campuses of the University of Hawaii, for example, have accepted the statement on professional ethics of the American Association of University Professors and are currently modifying their own harassment policies to indicate that sexual relationships between faculty/supervisors and students/employees, even by mutual consent, may be grounds for disciplinary action. Although the adoption of a code of professional ethics does not necessarily guarantee ethical behavior, it does demonstrate that a college is committed to ensuring an ethical academic community.

## Ethics in the Classroom

When a college clearly identifies its values, it will record those values that should actually guide it in the development of its mission, goals, philosophy, and operational procedures. Statements that illustrate the ways that values can be integrated into the operation of a college create a barometer that permits the institution to judge its progress and provide the president and upper-level administrators a basis upon which to evaluate their leadership. "The most reliable means college or university presidents have to ensure moral and ethical behavior from their staff and students is to provide clear guidelines (i.e. institutional values), personally model the behavior expected of others, and hold themselves open to judgment for ethical performance" (McCabe, 1991, pp. 19-20).

Many colleges may operate on the assumption that "as long as students are scheduled into classrooms with faculty, good things will happen" (McCabe, 1991, p. 2). But the concept of academic freedom presents an ethical issue that is seldom confronted. Faculty members who maintain that academic freedom means complete freedom to do anything they wish in the classroom often use this belief as the basis for resisting student evaluations, programs to improve the quality of instruction, or curricular developments consistent with an overall college plan.

Colleges and universities are ethically bound to be honest in their dealings with students. They should be compelled to tell students their expectations of moral standards, offer information in a timely manner and usable format, and provide frequent and objective feedback. "They should also have the same obligations to the faculty who teach those students, to the staff who must support the teaching/learning relationship, and to the administration that must create an appropriate environment to promote teaching/learning" (McCabe, 1991, pp. 16–17).

More closely related to the classroom than some of the issues already discussed are institutional procedures that fail to encourage responsibility. Allowing students to drop out of class without penalty and giving them nonpunitive grades, that is, substituting *withdrawn* or *no credit* for a failing grade, are examples of such procedures. These practices not only foster grade inflation and distortion in transferring credit between institutions but also may encourage students to take a casual approach to their studies. Are educators acting responsibly (and here *responsibly* implies a moral standard) when they allow students to drop out of instructional programs or courses at will or encourage them to make no advance commitments to complete a course they have enrolled in? Although these policies are less prevalent than they were in the 1960s, they have left their scars.

Other ethical issues plague the classroom also. Plagiarism, cheating, and the demotivation of students will be discussed in the following sections.

*Plagiarism*

Perhaps the best way of introducing the intractable issue of plagiarism is by describing a personal experience. Several years ago, a large federal agency asked me to review responses to the agency's request for proposals. Coincidentally, one of the responding proposals I reviewed contained several pages of unattributed comments that I myself had written earlier. The grant, needless to say, was not awarded to the solicitor.

While it is unlikely that this situation would occur often, it does point up the problem of failure to document material or provide proper attribution. Plagiarism occurs at all levels of the school system, but in all cases it is both a moral and pedagogical issue that can be addressed in the classroom by various approaches. McCormick (1989), for example, urges instructors to show students how to use secondary materials responsibly. Nienhuis (1989) describes a teaching approach derived from the observation of students' note-taking procedures and their subsequent involvement in the process. Brogan and Brogan (1982) note that since most scientific and engineering reports are not copyrighted, there is a growing tendency of people to adopt material from these reports in student papers as well as in professional reports and dissertations.

Plagiarism is not confined to the classroom or to educational institutions. It does not often result in legal exercises and decisions, but it can have serious implications for both the individuals involved and for society as a whole. In 1988, the failure to give proper attribution in a speech contributed to Senator Joseph Biden's withdrawing from the presidential race. In the same year, and for similar reasons, Richard J. Sauer withdrew his candidacy for president of North Dakota State University. Despite the prevailing guidelines for citing materials, some individuals genuinely may not understand that they are plagiarizing because they fail to understand the basis of footnoting or referencing: giving proper credit to writers whose work is used and providing reference for readers who want to explore the subject further (Skom, 1986).

## *Cheating*

Cheating in the classroom is closely aligned to plagiarism. Various methods may be employed to cope with this problem, and most instructors have their own special approaches. If students could be actively engaged in the learning process as well as in the results, perhaps cheating would diminish. In its own effort to eliminate cheating, the University of Maryland has produced a workable code of student conduct (Connell, 1981).

Positive modeling by teachers may be the best deterrent to cheating. If professors are open about their own work and give proper attribution for material from others, students may be less likely to cheat or to plagiarize written material.

Cheating cannot be tolerated because it is simply unethical. Even so, many students consider it wrong to report someone for cheating. This issue can be addressed by designing mechanisms that make it easy for them to report cheating anonymously, thus minimizing the risk of social ostracism and converting the students to a level of standards greater than that which binds them to their fellows. A mechanism for reporting cheating with minimal risk must be paired with a vigorous statement on the importance of not cheating because cheating undermines the college. This may be a difficult task since the hold of the peer group on students must be surmounted (Fass, 1990).

### Demotivating Students

Another issue that can be discussed in terms of ethics is the "demotivation" of students. During the fall of 1980, students at Nebraska Indian Community College, Macy Campus, identified key behaviors of community college instructors that they felt demotivated American Indian students. The top ten items were talking down to or ridiculing students, showing disinterest in students and their views and problems, asking for questions but never answering them, failing to return assignments or returning tests and other materials weeks after they were turned in, using concepts and classification categories that students had never heard of, playing favorites, grading unfairly, coming to class late or unprepared, and using lecture methods exclusively (Griffin, 1982). These types of negative behavior pertain to all ethnic groups, both genders, and every educational institution—from kindergarten to graduate school.

## Ethics and Administrative Issues

The federal guidelines for affirmative action establish the necessity of fair hiring practices for women and for previously underrepresented minorities. At the same time, they do not and in fact cannot guarantee fair hiring practices for those outside this mandate—white males in particular. Those who hire faculty members must develop and execute criteria that provide for the best instructors for the particular tasks at hand.

The fundamental issue in all affirmative action is the attempt to eliminate discrimination. Basically, the question is whether present hiring practices can or should be used to redress long-standing biases that kept women and nonwhites away from teaching or administrative positions. The problem is, "How does a society that espouses and appears to believe deeply in equality of opportunity for all people rid itself of the personal as well as structural barriers that cause inequality to prevail?" (Shavlik, 1990, p. 160).

Institutions must be careful of discriminating against well-qualified white males just for the sake of satisfying some short-term, politically charged issue of appointing role models for students of different races. Appointing role models for everyone is difficult because the protected classes include not only women and blacks but also Hispanics, Asians, and American Indians. And the problem goes further because of the various subcategories of Puerto Ricans, Cubans, and Mexicans and the more than twenty groups that the Census Bureau characterizes as Asian. At what point does a student body have sufficient numbers of a subgroup such that a role model must be appointed?

Shavlik points out that "the people in institutions should meet frequently in an effort to understand the legacy of discrimination, to explore the need for change, and to build a comprehensive model for change" (1990, pp. 165–166). Much of the current problem is due to the fact that the models for excellence in the faculty ranks are such that certain ethical behaviors seem aberrant. In community colleges, the models for excellence are severely limited if an instructor is expected to do little more than to show up for class and get the grades in on time. It is this model that should come into question.

Years after the Title IX education amendment was to have ended discrimination against women in colleges and universities, women administrators and faculty members in community colleges still believe that de facto sex discrimination is being practiced on their campuses. Despite the plethora of anecdotes and individual tales of gender-based devaluation, factual evidence to support the perceptions of institutionalized discrimination against women has been lacking. Many people still continue to believe that discrimination did not and does not exist, a view that is persistent, damaging to morale, and counterproductive. Data support the claims of discrimination in terms of types of jobs, promotions, and salaries, but the data on affirmative action may not reveal hidden patterns of gender discrimination (Weeks and Wygan, 1990).

In San Francisco, community advisory committees for various cultural and ethnic communities provide input to educational planning processes and also serve as conduits to the respective communities. They make an effort to ensure that a multicultural, multiethnic community college such as San Francisco Community College can include people of many backgrounds who can work together despite conflicts. Awareness of the differences between cultural and ethnic backgrounds is one way of understanding these differences (Hsu, 1990).

## Conclusion

Even though much attention has been focused on medical and business ethics in higher education in the past twenty years, the ethics of colleges themselves have warranted less discussion. Ethical questions seemed to be confined to matters of social responsibility, such as sexual harassment, and to isolated questions of propriety in athletic programs, student cheating and plagiarism, and student evaluations. More recently, that list has been expanded to include issues in scientific research, multicultural and ethnic relations, academic planning, racism on campus, and free speech by student groups.

But the broader issues of just how the college should respond to ethical dilemmas are rarely discussed as a total enterprise. More likely, colleges have been following a general notion that suggests that colleges and universities will act fairly, will be fully aware of the consequences of their actions, and will accept accountability.

Questions abound about what criteria and scales should be used to measure fairness and what people should be considered in these measurements. The few attempts to address these questions are generally relegated to the research universities. Although community colleges are not driven by the quest for research, they could engage in moral discourse by considering what they should be doing after fulfilling their mission of access. After all, they have already enrolled nearly everyone they can entice onto their campuses. The time is past due for them to decide what their stance should be as moral institutions. Education is a morally charged enterprise, but since the reservoir of public trust in higher education is quickly drying up, there should be substantive discourse on moral issues without confrontations and ultimatums. This discourse might occur through student seminar programs and through interchanges with faculty members and administrators.

More clearly defined advertising and selection criteria for staffing are other means by which colleges can demonstrate responsibility. If an advertisement says, "Women and minorities are strongly encouraged to apply," should white males not bother to apply? Or is this wording mere rhetoric? Ethical insensitivity in hiring faculty members also becomes obvious when one hundred or two hundred applications come in and no individual or group is given sufficient time to review them carefully or time to return a personal message to each applicant pointing out why the application did not receive a favorable response. The ethical institution would so respond to everyone who applied, and it would not invite a candidate to visit merely to fulfill an affirmative action mandate if the candidate is not to be given a realistic hearing.

Clearly enunciating criteria for behavior and spelling out expectations—for teaching and learning, hiring and evaluating faculty, and personal conduct—are mandatory for colleges as they enter a new decade. We can learn from our early history. Colleges must again become institutions of responsibility and ethical, exemplary conduct.

## References

Adorno, T. W., Frenkel-Brunswik, E., Levinson, D. J., and Sanford, N. *The Authoritarian Personality.* New York: HarperCollins, 1950.

Brogan, K. M., and Brogan, J. D. "Yet Another Ethical Problem in Technical Writing." Paper presented at the 13th annual meeting of the College English Association, Houston, Apr. 1982. (ED 229 782)

Brunner, R. B. "Legal, Societal, and Ethical Issues Concerning Intellectual Rights in Computer Education." Paper presented at the 13th annual meeting of the Society of Scholars and Educators, Miami Shores, Florida, Oct. 1988. (ED 299 678)

Clarke, C. "Integrating Ethics in Community Colleges' Accounting Programs." *Community Review, 1989-1990*, 1990, *12*(1-2), 13-18. (EJ 418 730)

Cohen, A. M. "The Faculty Member as Recluse." Keynote speech presented at the Seventh Annual International Institute on the Community College, Sarnia, Canada, June 1976. (ED 125 681)

Cohen, A. M., and Brawer, F. B. *Confronting Identity: The Community College Instructor.* Englewood Cliffs, N.J.: Prentice-Hall, 1972.

Cohen, A. M., and Brawer, F. B. *The Two-Year College Instructor Today.* Troy, Mo.: Holt, Rinehart & Winston, 1977.

Cohen, A. M., and Brawer, F. B. *The Collegiate Function of Community Colleges: Fostering Higher Learning Through Curriculum and Student Transfer.* San Francisco: Jossey-Bass, 1987.

Cohen, A. M., and Brawer, F. B. *The American Community College.* (2nd ed.) San Francisco: Jossey-Bass, 1989.

Connell, C. "Term Paper Mills Continue to Grind." *Educational Record*, 1981, *62*(3), 19-28. (EJ 252 357)

Dziech, B. W. "Colleges Must Help to Improve the Bewildering Complexities of Sexual Harassment." *Chronicle of Higher Education*, Nov. 13, 1991, *38*(12), B1, B3.

Dziech, B. W., and Weiner, L. *The Lecherous Professor: Sexual Harassment on Campus.* Boston: Beacon Press, 1984.

Edmonson, W. F. "Requiring Ethics Instruction in Community and Junior Colleges: A Mission Unfulfilled," 1989. (ED 305 099)

Fass, R. A. "Cheating and Plagiarism." In W. W. May (ed.), *Ethics and Higher Education.* New York: American Council on Education/Macmillan, 1990.

Gottleber, T. T. "Teaching Ethics in the Community College Data Processing Curriculum." *Community/Junior College Quarterly of Research and Practice*, 1988, *12*(1), 47-54. (EJ 369 314)

Griffin, W. A., Jr. "How Instructors Demotivate the American Indian Community College Student: A Report of a Survey at Nebraska Indian Community College, Macy Campus, 1980-1981," 1982. (ED 213 565)

Hoiles, J. A. "Ethics in the Business Curriculum at the Community College." Princeton, N.J.: Princeton University Mid-Career Fellowship Program, 1989. (ED 307 935)

Hsu, H. "The Multicultural Urban Community College: Conflict and Achievement." Paper presented at Leadership 2,000, the 2nd annual International Conference on Leadership Development of the League for Innovation in Community Colleges, San Francisco, July 1990. (ED 322 966)

Laney, J. T. "Through Thick and Thin: Two Ways of Talking About the Academy and Moral Responsibility." In W. W. May (ed.), *Ethics and Higher Education.* New York: American Council on Education/Macmillan, 1990.

Little, D. "Addressing the Issue of Appropriate Professional Ethics on Community College Campuses." Paper presented at the 69th annual convention of the American Association of Community and Junior Colleges, Washington, D.C., Mar.-Apr. 1989. (ED 306 999)

McCabe, R. H. "Educational Programs." Unpublished paper, Miami-Dade Community College, 1991.

McCormick, F. "The Plagiario and the Professor in Our Peculiar Institution." *Journal of Teaching-Writing,* 1989, *8*(2), 135-143. (EJ 410 112)

Nienhuis, T. "The Quick Fix: Curing Plagiarism with a Note-Taking Exercise." *College Teaching,* 1989, *37*(3), 100. (EJ 395 360)

Parsons, M. H. "Community Colleges and Civic Literacy: The Quest for Values, Ethics, and College Renewal." Paper presented at the annual convention of the Virginia Community Colleges, Roanoke, Virginia, Oct. 1989. (ED 314 104)

Parsons, M. H., and Powell, A. R. *Ethics and the Profession: An Assessment of the Eighties.* Hagerstown, Md.: Center for Public Policy Studies, Hagerstown Junior College, 1988. (ED 304 201)

Roediger, J. "Research and Development for a Course in Ethics in Nursing Practice for Community College Associate Degree Nursing Students." Olympia, Washington: South Puget Sound Community College, 1984. (ED 255 657)

Shavlik, D. "Affirmative Action: Solution or Problem?" In W. W. May (ed.), *Ethics and Higher Education.* New York: American Council on Education/Macmillan, 1990.

Skom, E. "Plagiarism: Quite a Rather Bad Little Crime." *AAHE Bulletin,* 1986.

Small, M. J. "The Guardian of Heloise? Sexual Harassment in Higher Education." In W. W. May (ed.), *Ethics and Higher Education.* New York: American Council on Education/Macmillan, 1990.

Waller, W. "What Teaching Does to Teachers." In M. Hein, A. Vidich, and D. W. White (eds.), *Identity and Anxiety.* New York: Free Press, 1960.

Weeks, A. A., and Wygan, D. C. "Perceptions of Gender Discrimination: A Community College Case Study." In C. G. Sullivan (ed.), *Journal of the American Association of Women in Community and Junior Colleges.* Washington, D.C.: American Association of Community and Junior Colleges, 1990. (ED 319 424)

Whisnant, W. T. "Ethics and Administration in America's Community Colleges." *Community/Junior College Quarterly of Research and Practice,* 1988, *12*(3), 243–249. (EJ 379 121)

Wright, R. A. "Teaching Professional Ethics: Proceed, but with Caution." In A. D. Rassweiler and J. W. Hylander (eds.), *Proceedings of the Community College Humanities Association.* Cranford, N.J.: Union County College Press, 1985. (ED 259 812)

━━━━ **Chapter Five** ━━━━

# Academic Scruples:
# Faculty and Personnel Issues

## Joseph N. Hankin

General Omar Bradley once remarked, "The world has achieved brilliance without conscience. Ours is a world of nuclear giants and ethical infants." In 1986, as if to test this hypothesis, the Milton Bradley Company introduced a new board game called "A Question of Scruples." It became popular with college students, in part, because it addresses daily moral dilemmas. The players ask themselves ethical questions such as:

> Your teenage children ask if you ever smoked marijuana. You did. Do you admit it?
> By mistake, a large department store has failed to bill your account for a VCR. Do you notify the store?
> You are buying a house from an old lady. She is asking far too little. Do you tell her?
> As a famous athlete you are offered $100,000 to endorse a product you'd never use. What to do?
> In a parking lot you accidentally dent a car. Do you leave a note?

The game poses 252 such dilemmas on ethical problems of "everyday morality," including business, friendship, sex, romance, marriage, child rearing, aiding strangers, politics, helping the poor, returning excess change, and more. Each player gives a different answer, but the winner is not the one who answers "correctly," but rather the one who best anticipates the reactions of the other players.

Community college students, many of whom are older than university students and have been out in the "real world," may have faced more moral problems by the time they attend college than their grandparents faced in a lifetime. This game makes them and other players face up to the possibility that they or their friends might lie for what they consider to be perfectly good reasons.

This chapter provides a similar set of problems for community college administrators, members of the professoriate, and the professional reader with an interest in the ethical dilemmas faced by members of the college community. This set of problems, which is found at the end of the chapter and in examples in the text, might be used by an institution conducting an "ethics audit" to provoke discussion about specific dilemmas that it has faced or could face. (The ethics audit will be described more fully in a later section of this chapter.)

### Ethics in Academe

Society as a whole is faced continually with moral dilemmas, as Gardner (1978, p. 29) reminds us. "The majority of twentieth-century Americans continue with enthusiasm the old human preoccupation with what is 'right' and 'wrong.' Consider the successful effort to outlaw child labor in the early decades of this century, the fight to give women the vote, the struggle to abolish the sweatshop, the long campaign against racial and religious prejudice. Consider the gas chambers, slave-labor camps, My Lai, the torturing of political dissidents. In all cases the issues are moral, and the appropriate reaction is moral outrage—but in deference to twentieth-century sensibilities the word 'moral' is almost never uttered."

Yet despite the continual presence of serious moral dilemmas of a public nature, many people feel that current-day students and faculty members, indeed society itself, may be confused about ethics. Some even date this confusion to the time of Watergate, when Jeb Stuart Magruder said at the time of his sentencing for his part in the plot, "Somewhere between my ideals and ambitions, I lost my ethical compass" ("Boy Scout Without a Compass," 1974, p. 14).

In higher education, interest in ethics has taken several forms, including the establishment of a Society for Values in Higher Education in New Haven, Connecticut. The society has among its fellows faculty members at over four hundred colleges and universities. Several professional associations have published statements on professional ethics, including the American Association of University Professors and the American Association of State Colleges and Universities. In 1990, the Presidents Academy of the American Association of Community and Junior Colleges circulated a draft of an ethics statement for presidents to consider. This statement was approved in principle by the association in 1991 and was subsequently disseminated to community colleges throughout the nation.

Community college faculty members and students have also participated in this recent movement toward greater recognition of ethics. For instance, Bernadine McCollum, of Paradise Valley Community College in Arizona, introduces exercises on ethics into her classes to demonstrate that "ethics is not just a one-time, important business decision made by a high-level executive, but rather an accumulation of day-to-day, small-scale decisions made at all levels" (McCollum, 1990, p. 2). She varies the exercise, posing a question about an employee stealing and selling bicycles for cash and then asking the class if its decision might change if the employee had stolen only one bicycle and given it to an impoverished child for Christmas. She believes that "all instructors can supplement and reinforce the formal courses by integrating ethics into their routine course content" (p. 2).

During the period from 1987 to 1990, faculty and staff members at Middlesex County College in New Jersey attempted to build considerations of ethics into many sectors of campus life through the Ethics Project. Using a series of films, speakers, panel discussions, and faculty seminars, the project deliberately educates faculty, staff, and administrators on how to introduce ethical considerations into curriculum and campus administration ("College Puts Ethics on Front Burner," 1990).

Mellert (1990) writes about a similar emphasis on ethics at Brookdale Community College in New Jersey. "In many academic institutions . . . the three 'Rs' are recruitment, retention, and revenue. . . . We have been giving some attention to the fourth 'R,' responsibility" (p. 1). The institution has developed a way of involving interested faculty members in discussions of ethical questions, which will be described later in this chapter.

However, in most of the literature about ethics in higher education, community colleges seem to have been left out. For instance, not one of the twenty-eight authors in a book recently published by the American Council on Education, *Ethics and Higher Education* (May, 1990), was currently at a community college. Hence, the book deals with matters such as the conflict between the need for faculty members to produce scholarly articles and their teaching assignments and the lack of effective affirmative action in hiring practices, issues that are treated quite differently in community colleges.

Although faculty members may feel ambiguous or confused about their role in specific ethical dilemmas, in some respects academe is quite clear about ethics: 89 percent of two-year college faculty members in a 1989 study believe it "fairly" or "very" important to shape the values of their students (The Carnegie Foundation for the Advancement of Teaching, 1989, p. 9). About 79 percent of this same group rate their institution's performance in shaping values as adequate or better than adequate.

Unfortunately, most of the effort to deal with ethics on community college campuses occurs within the context of the instructional program. Although this emphasis is well and good, faculty and staff members need to pay more attention to their own ethical obligations to students as well as to the institution. Unless institutional leaders encourage ethical awareness, current practices will persist. To avoid unethical practices, institutional leaders must make it a top priority to create and maintain a campus environment that encourages discussion—even confrontation. When people are afraid to speak out, they will not speak out. When people believe their actions will go unnoticed, they will be less likely to hold themselves accountable.

Faculty members are clear on some ethical dilemmas in their lives, but these waters can get muddy too. The key question is, If no one were watching you, or if you knew you would not be punished, would you as a faculty member be tempted to cheat to pass a test, face a jail sentence to make a lot of money, inflate a conference expense report, lie on an income tax return, exaggerate on an insurance damage report, distort the truth to achieve a professional objective, or accept a gift from a textbook publisher or materials supplier? Individuals might react differently to each of these situations, depending on circumstances.

What is the role of the role model in an institution of higher education? Faculty members serve as role models to students (and occasionally to one another). The faculty members' supervisors are role models to the faculty members, the administrators to the supervisors, and the board to the administration. Where does this chain begin and end?

What are the proper roles of community college staff and faculty members? Do they take positions of leadership even when their actions may not be popular with their students and colleagues? Can the individual faculty member go against the "mob mentality"? Do community colleges merely reflect local values?

Oliver Wendell Holmes suggested that colleges are marketplaces of ideas. If there are competing goods or even conflicting interests in the community college, which should prevail? How do we deal with conflicting values? A faculty member might react in many different ways to breaches in ethics, saying, for example, "I won't report her because she might report me." "I won't report her because she might not like me." "I won't report her because, after all, she is a dean." "Although I disagree with his action, I will uphold his right to have his own views." "There is no way I can force myself to do something I consider morally wrong."

Should colleagues support each other against the students or the administration whether or not they are behaving correctly? In other words, do faculty members close ranks no matter what?

How can the faculty and administration create an environment on campus that leads faculty members to establish, maintain, and follow ethical principles? What are those principles? Can faculty members and administrators agree on those principles?

Not all of these issues will be resolved in this chapter. But it is enough to identify them so that they can serve as topics for discussion by readers.

Faculty members do discuss issues involving ethics in a variety of ways, but how closely are those discussions related to real life? Typically, the discussions of ethics on many college campuses are limited to issues in class such as removal of a patient from a respirator, genetics research, and the ethical responsibilities of the modern-day international corporation trading abroad and giving bribes to prospective buyers. Students in these discussions become proficient at considering the dilemmas faced by institutions and even legislators. However, most community college students and faculty members will never have to select a candidate for an organ transplant or issue the order that sends a murderer to the electric chair. They will, however, need to be able to function in real-life situations.

Community college leaders, then, need to communicate to the campus community the standards and values they expect to see reflected in everything that everyone at the institution does. They have the primary responsibility for creating a climate in which faculty and staff members speak and act ethically as opposed to expediently. Indeed, faculty and staff members must view speaking out, especially on ethical issues, not only as a right but as a responsibility.

One way of creating a climate on campus conducive to open discussion of ethical issues is to promote active and ongoing discussions of standards and values at general meetings and in special groups. These discussions should center on serious but common situations that faculty and staff members face, such as the examples presented in this chapter. The characters, responsibilities, and options in these situations may not be at all clear cut, and their decisions and actions may be questionable. For many situations, there may be no single acceptable solution. But in the process of analyzing the ethical dilemmas, faculty and staff members are forced to confront and examine their own principles and values and weigh them against possible conflicting values and expectations inherent in institutional policies, procedures, and professional standards.

Participants in the discussions increase their understanding of the complexities that arise when two or more competing interests or sets of standards come into conflict. This understanding leads to more thoughtful and, one hopes, more ethical behavior among members of the campus community. And because the discussions also serve as opportunities for campus leaders to communicate their commitment to the highest ethical standards at their institution, the discussions should reduce people's fear of speaking out and increase the fear of acting immorally or unethically. Once a climate exists that promotes open debate on ethical issues, the institution is well on its way to including ethical issues as a part of the institutional culture.

### Six Examples of Ethical Dilemmas

The following six examples represent the kinds of ethical dilemmas that faculty and staff members should discuss. They are highly developed versions of situations similar to those provided at the end of the chapter. They illustrate how these situations can be expanded for discussion. One example has been included for each subsection of situations.

In these six situations, readers will recognize situations they themselves have faced in their careers or that they have watched develop and explode around them at one time or another. Each of the situations ends with one or more questions whose answers often depend on how confident participants feel about the support or repercussions they might encounter as a result of their chosen action. Hence, debating these dilemmas will reveal as much about the ethical climate of the institution as it will about the principles and values of the group members. Participants may explore these dilemmas in a variety of public sessions and may use role playing as a way of exploring the issues inherent in the dilemmas.

#### Ethical Dilemma in Student Services

John Able, a serious and intense student, visited his counselor, Sue Berry, one Friday afternoon. In the course of the session, he revealed his enmity for a neighbor. In fact, as was developed later in an attention-getting trial, he said that he was going to kill the neighbor, Bill Chase. Sue repeated none of this conversation, not even to her supervisor, the director of counseling, Mary Duncan, or to the dean of students, Don Ealing, because she knew the college's policy that counseling sessions with students were to be treated as privileged and confidential. Sue had been a counselor for three years, beginning right out of graduate school. Her training had not prepared her for a situation such as this. She did not feel she could even ask her colleagues for advice.

Instead, she decided to wait until after the weekend and call John in to discuss further his feelings and the threat. However, on Saturday evening, John Able killed Bill Chase after a violent argument and was immediately apprehended. It was only then that Sue went to her supervisor. Mary Duncan, after conferring with Don Ealing, suggested to Sue that she not volunteer any information, lest the college and she herself be blamed for the death. Mary said that if pressed, Sue should consult the college's attorney before responding. She advised Sue not to write up the whole affair as Sue was inclined to do from her notes and even to consider destroying the notes.

Sue was in a quandary. Should she consult with the dean's superior, the president? What if he felt as the others did? What if he decided not to give her tenure because she was unsupportive?

The family of Bill Chase sued the college to obtain the records on John Able on the chance that they would reveal something about the reasons behind his death. The president, who was briefed by the others, told Sue in no uncertain terms how to testify. She was represented by the college's attorney, who gave her further instructions. But under the pressures of the trial, she told all she knew. The college settled with the family for a seven-figure sum. What would you do if you were one of the participants?

### Ethical Dilemma in Curricula

Carole Glynn is a tenured member of a department that offers remedial reading. She overheard a conversation between Milt Hoskins and Elizabeth Isaacs, two senior members of the department who had been charged with developing a report on the effectiveness of the program in preparing students for further college work. They had, quite properly, consulted the entire department in designing the study that was to compare the students' test scores and grades before and after taking the department's courses. The study was to establish whether students who took the courses persisted in college in greater numbers than those who did not and whether the subsequent grades earned by successful participants were better than those of students who either did not take the courses or who did poorly in them. But the two researchers were falsifying their results.

Carole, upon learning that her two colleagues were falsifying the results of the study, went to her chairperson, Wilhelmina von Jaeger. Wilhelmina had been instrumental in designing and developing the college's program of remediation, one that had since been copied by many other community colleges. Although professing to be shocked by Carole's findings, the chairperson counseled Carole to keep the information private and let her take care of the report. Her parting words to her younger colleague were "Remember, you are up for promotion to associate professor this year, and you don't want to make enemies now."

In reviewing the final report when it came out, Carole realized that nothing had been done to correct the false data. The report was used in the college's assessment report to the state and in the self-study required by the regional accrediting body prior to re-accreditation of the institution. Carole considered going to the dean or the president. What would you do if you were one of the participants?

### Ethical Dilemma in Instructional Activities

Marc Karl shares an office with Bob Leland, and they frequently discuss students they have had. Marc had given Jessica McMann a C in the fall semester, and Bob was now considering her final grade for the spring. He told Marc that he was going to give her a D because she was a "pain in the neck," which Marc knew from first-hand experience to be true. Marc said nothing, but thought, Bob's going to get us all in trouble for that, because he knew that Jessica's father was a town supervisor and an influential person in the community.

Predictably, Jessica appealed the grade, going through the proper channels—seeing Bob and then the department chairperson, Greg Noonan. Greg's position was that Bob was correct. The next step was to call into session a collegewide hearing group that would advise Dean Leslie Oxbow, who would make the final decision. The hearing group, which had begun meeting on such matters in 1965, consisted of an equal number of students, faculty members, and administrators. Group members were not happy because they had to meet after commencement, but they listened attentively to both sides and rendered a decision. The grade was not changed. In the fall when Marc returned, he learned of the decision and knew that, had he testified, the student would have been upheld.

The student's father started to get some of his political colleagues upset, and there was talk that the budget of the college might not pass because of this one simple act now blessed by institutional support. Marc had no desire to be a whistle-blower, but he made an appointment with the president, Fred Preston, to apprise him of the facts as he knew them and to offer support in the upcoming budget deliberations. What would you do if you were one of the participants?

### Ethical Dilemma in Personnel Matters

Lester Quick, chairperson of the philosophy department at a large urban community college, calls his counterpart at another community college. The chairperson is out, and the secretary asks Alfred Rohrer for a reference on Sam Steele, a member of the department and a long-time colleague. Rohrer is startled. He knows that Sam has recently been charged with sexually harassing several female students. He may not be guilty, but Rohrer has heard rumors about Sam's activities ever since the death of his wife three years ago.

Philosophy jobs are not easy to come by, and Rohrer does not want to ruin his colleague's chances of employment in a new setting. Furthermore, last year the newspapers carried stories about a community college that was successfully sued because an individual's reputation had been damaged by careless, though true, remarks. Rohrer hems and haws and answers most of Lester's questions quickly and in short sentences. Then comes the final question, "Can you think of any reason why we should not employ Professor Steele or why you would not if he were a new applicant to your community college?" Rohrer feebly says, "No . . . but maybe you should speak with our chairperson, Dr. Dolan," and politely completes the call. Under what obligation is a faculty colleague or Dr. Dolan, the chairperson, to alert other prospective employing institutions of Sam Steele's alleged actions when called for a reference? What would you do if you were one of the participants?

### Ethical Dilemma in Governance and Relations Between the College and the Community

Laura Thompson is on the faculty senate of a community college and also substituted as the institution's representative in the last meeting of a statewide faculty council of community colleges. At that meeting, she learned about the new consumer legislation and was persuaded that the college has an ethical obligation to report information concerning campus security to the public. She also knows that she has little influence and would be the first to be let go from her department in a budget cutback.

The chairperson of the faculty senate, Ruth Ungar, sends these consumer regulations to a committee to "deep six" them and avoid undue publicity. Thompson suspects that Ungar has done so with the full consent—even encouragement—of the administration. A small group of faculty members cares about such matters and wants to go to the dean to discuss the next step. But before they approach the dean, a reporter for a local newspaper appears on campus and asks for the security reports showing crime statistics for the past year. She is told that such reports do not exist, but Thompson knows that they do. What would you do if you were one of the participants?

### Ethical Dilemma in Budget and Finance

A group of county legislators threatens a college financially because it disagrees with art work hung in the college gallery, a play performed at the school, and curriculum material in a human sexuality class. Brian Vesey is asking for an important sum of money in the budget. His request is not in jeopardy because he is in a science department, far removed from the departments responsible for the offending practices. A legislator, "Wild Bill" Williamson, sees him in the grocery store and asks his opinion about what is going on. Secretly, Vesey disagrees with the critics and knows the faculty members responsible are not especially radical, but he wants to leave the impression of agreeing with Williamson so that Wild Bill will not go after Vesey's own pet project. Giving a noncommittal answer, Vesey tells Williamson that he should talk with the dean and president and maybe even the trustees about this rash of incidents. What would you do if you were one of the participants?

### The Ethics Audit

The concept of an ethics audit is advanced by Daniel H. Perlman (1990), among others. The ethics audit attempts to determine what students, faculty members, and staff members value.

How many institutions have recently conducted an audit, through campuswide discussions, of what students value in professors? And have these institutions tried to reconcile this list with the list of activities of their professors? For instance, if most students admire faculty members who are up-to-date in the scholarship of their discipline but a particular professor is obviously not up-to-date, what can the institution do? What should the institution do? Similarly, if students value personal relationships with professors but such relationships are not available—or, perhaps, are too available—what should the institution do?

Institutions with an interest in fostering discussion on ethical matters might sponsor a lecture series on some of the questions evolving from the cases in this chapter or on the potential conflict between institutional, personal, and academic values, as suggested by Laney (1990). Robert Mellert (1990) details what Brookdale Community College in New Jersey does to provoke discussion on ethical matters: it canvases the entire college community for issues involving ethics and then, based upon the returns, schedules discussions and role-playing sessions to highlight the dilemmas that campus citizens face.

Mellert points out that "it is important that ethical discussion be based upon issues that are of genuine interest at any given time on campus" (1990, p. 1). Margaret J. Barr, discussing ethical standards as they might apply to students on a specific campus, cautions that "each academic community must determine the appropriate standard for its unique context" (Barr, 1990, p. 279).

What happens, however, if there is little or no response when a campus is canvased for examples of ethical problems? Mellert (1990), in his first attempt to canvas his campus, received only nineteen replies from two hundred appeals. In such a case, a professional or an institution might well use the situations given at the end of this chapter to start the campuswide discussions. Different colleges, with different concerns, could select from the list those situations that were of particular concern or that could provoke the greatest discussion. These situations might educate the campus community on the range of issues available, expose people to situations they would not have thought of themselves, make people aware that they might not be able to predict the responses of colleagues, and set the stage for a series of subdiscussions among different groups (board and president, faculty and administration, students and faculty) that could be held all year long if the institution were dedicated to a full exploration of the topic.

Because unethical conduct is often due to a lack of awareness or understanding of ethical standards, discussions like these could well sensitize the campus community to various issues. If nothing more comes from them than sensitizing the campus community, the discussions will have been worthwhile. However, some institutions might want to go further and establish codes of conduct, lists of prohibited and acceptable behavior, and even processes to deal with ethical lapses. At the very least, institutions that consider themselves collegial could do a great deal to further this self-image by considering the range of ethical issues in this chapter.

## The Ethical Dilemmas

The ethical dilemmas were designed to focus the reader's concerns on real-life issues. The reader will notice that answers to these dilemmas and even the dilemmas themselves are not always clear cut; there are many gray areas. Often, several ameliorating actions are possible. Some people may even question whether all of the examples given are really ethical dilemmas. Some of them seem political as well as ethical. Some of the examples are basic and seem to call for simple commonsense answers, at least on the surface. They are included, nonetheless, because at some institutions of higher education, even the simple issues require further discussion. Some of the dilemmas could be placed in more than one category; for example, sexual discrimination is included in an ethical dilemma under the categories of instructional activities and personnel matters. Some issues, like censorship and academic freedom, are fairly clear cases. Others are not so clear. They may make the reader wonder, Where do we draw the line? Who is responsible for what? For example, not every two-year college is unionized and not all have collegial processes for discussing dilemmas such as those posed.

The ethical dilemmas are based on situations that have occurred on community college campuses. Readers will recognize a number of them in one form or another. In evaluating the issues and attempting to solve the dilemmas associated with each example, readers will likely come face-to-face with their own value systems, and come to recognize just how important it is to face the dilemmas forthrightly while realizing the difficulty of finding solutions.

## Ethical Dilemmas in Student Services

You, an admissions counselor, admit a student who has a learning disability when you know that your college has few or no services specifically designed to deal with people with learning disabilities or other special needs. Your community college continues to advertise that it is fully accessible to these groups.

Your colleague counsels female students to enter "safe" fields rather than those not traditionally open to women, arguing from personal conviction that they "should not get their hopes up." You observe this behavior over time, and you want to report her to the supervising administrator but are fearful of reprisals.

A faculty member learns that one of his students has been raped by another student and later uses this information against her. His colleagues, not wanting to get involved, look the other way. You, a female member of the department, do not want to drop the issue. With the permission of the student, you report the incident to the associate dean. She is horrified but is fearful that such news will damage the college and perhaps her chances of getting the newly opened position at a nearby institution.

As a faculty adviser to a student organization, you learn that your student leaders are planning something illegal. You try to convince the group's members that they should refrain from their planned actions but do not succeed in doing so. Being a product of the 1960s yourself, you are somewhat taken with the idea but also realize its clear illegality.

You, a golf coach, realize that the country club that permits your team to use its course for practice for free discriminates in its membership against minority groups. One year, you notice a promising young black golfer, but to develop his talent might mean the loss of the privileges at the country club for the entire team.

You believe that an athletic coach falsified grades of her players to be able to play an ineligible player in order to win. What if the administration found out? Should it press for her removal as a coach or a faculty member?

You ask yourself, Can the college truly divorce itself from damage done by its student athletes to a landlord's premises when the institution takes no responsiblity for finding athletes housing in the community? What if the college allows the coaches to help the students find the housing to begin with? What if the college just permits such housing to be listed on its bulletin boards?

### Ethical Dilemmas in Curricula

How ethical is it for a faculty member to fail to keep current in his or her field? Is it ethical for the faculty member's colleagues or superiors to permit this to happen? If a colleague is only temporarily lazy, you feel that you might understand the lapse. But what if the offending party thinks her courses are colorful because the lecture notes are yellowing? Who has what responsibility?

The syllabus for a course overemphasizes a Eurocentric view, but you, an individual faculty member, have a broader worldview. Despite your pleadings, the department refuses to change the curriculum or syllabus largely because to do so correctly would require a major overhaul, and senior members of the department just do not want to bother. You feel so strongly about the issue that you want to call this to the attention of the college administration.

A college decides on English as a second language rather than bilingualism in its approach to new immigrant students. You, a faculty member from the same cultural group as the new students, disagree.

A faculty committee decides that it is not in agreement with the long-standing mission of the noncredit community services area of the college. It also finds that nowhere in the state law is there a sanction for the two other major functions of the college, transfer and occupational education. The committee introduces a resolution onto the floor of the faculty governing body that calls for a drastic cutback in noncredit community services, which the committee sees as "cheapening" the college. You are the leader of the generally respected faculty governing body.

Local community leaders oppose offering high school equivalency and adult basic education at your community college. As a new faculty member, you are interested in offering these programs because you have analyzed census data that show a real need for the programs. You suspect racism as the underlying cause of the opposition. One of the community leaders tells you to "stick to your last" and ignore the obvious community need.

You are a faculty member who is employed during the summer months by a nearby industrial plant. During the year, a curriculum decision concerning the offering of training at that same plant comes before a departmental committee, and you represent the deciding vote. Should you make known your connection before voting?

The recreation leadership curriculum, offered by your department, is popular with student athletes. However, recent surveys clearly show that high school students can obtain positions in the field without college study. Members of the department know this, but they need to enroll the students in order to justify their courses.

### Ethical Dilemmas in Instructional Activities

A student advisee of yours comes in during the first week of class to change course sections. His assigned professor has told everyone in the overcrowded section that half of those who remain in the course will flunk and that his students will be assigned backbreaking amounts of work. You suspect the professor has done this to lower the size of his class section.

A colleague of yours has a strict attendance policy for students in her class. Yet you observe that she violates it herself by using up her sick days throughout the semester, frequently on Fridays or Mondays, without announcing her absence in advance to the class.

Your colleague constantly arrives just before his class begins, parks illegally in a handicapped parking spot, lets the class go five minutes early each and every day, does not hold office hours, and is otherwise disrespectful of the rules of the college. You know about this behavior because students of yours also have him as an instructor, and they confide in you.

A faculty member catches measles, but comes in to teach her part-time classes for overload pay anyway. She professes to be too ill to teach her full-time classes, for which she automatically is paid sick leave. When you tell her that she is endangering her students, she shrugs and says, "I can't afford to have them miss too much material. Besides, they should get the illness when they are young anyway. I didn't and now see how I am suffering."

A faculty member comes to you to ask you for all your unused copies of textbooks. It seems he has been collecting them from other colleagues too in order to sell them at the college's bookstore.

A faculty member allows a teaching assistant to do too much actual instruction, claiming that she is giving him needed experience. You, her office mate, are aware that the faculty member is taking advantage of the class and of the teaching assistant.

A secretary who is supposed to aid in preparing instructional materials is used by a faculty member in a private enterprise. You observe this happening.

A union contract requires a majority vote by the department before any educational innovation can be introduced. A new faculty member, eager to teach well, seeks such a vote. The vote fails, yet the faculty member introduces the innovation anyway. You, the chairperson of the department, are sympathetic with both points of view, and are caught in the middle.

You know that a colleague is copying materials—chapters from books, video- and audiotapes, and computer programs—that are protected legally from copyright infringement. Your college may be liable for damages for permitting such practices.

You know that your office mate at your college is engaging in research on students in violation of federal, state, and institutional rules governing such research.

If your community college is asked by a labor union or a company to train union members for a field that will exclude others on grounds other than incompetence, should it do so?

If a hospital will not employ members of minority groups, should the community college use it as a clinical facility? If the same hospital offers prospective employees a scholarship in exchange for a guaranteed job, but restricts the scholarship de facto to individuals from only one racial group, should the college join in the scholarship program?

A student in a class comes to you, her faculty adviser, and complains that another student is having an affair with the teacher. The student feels that the other members of the class may be at a disadvantage in regard to grades but is reluctant to file an official complaint because she fears reprisal.

What do you, the faculty supervisor, do with an experienced teacher who may be grading too easily in a class she teaches? What if the faculty member does this from a misguided sense of doing good; that is, she knows that poor grades will keep the students from obtaining a scholarship or even from graduating? You wrestle with the question: Who maintains the institutional obligation to keep standards high?

### *Ethical Dilemmas in Personnel Matters*

You are the chairperson of the affirmative action committee. Your group is trying to decide the ethical position of the institution toward underrepresented employee groups. You know that one department is considering employing an individual who is less than fully competent in order to meet affirmative action goals. You consider bringing this question to the next meeting of your committee: When two such standards are found in juxtaposition to one another, who is the arbiter?

An experienced faculty member says he is a Native American on the application for a research grant to improve his chances of obtaining it. He is not a Native American. At first this was done tongue-in-cheek, but as the award appears more and more of a certainty, you, a colleague, consider turning him in.

A faculty member suddenly announces that she earned her doctorate at Erewhon University and asks to have a salary increase and have the degree listed in the college catalogue. You, her chairperson, cannot find the whereabouts of this particular university to verify her transcript. Upon further inquiry, you determine that her transcript is from a "diploma mill." When confronted, the faculty member says, "Why accost me? You let Professor Conundrum get away with it last year!" Needless to say, you were not aware of the ruse last year.

A faculty member earns a doctorate, but you, his chairperson, know the research was plagiarized. You inform the administration and learn that it does not want the adverse publicity from the case at this time. The granting institution would revoke the degree if it knew of the fraud. What obligations do you and your college have in these circumstances?

You believe that your department is deliberately overusing part-time faculty members to save money and possibly to keep the additional class sections for full-time faculty members. You have not taught such a section in years and have no desire to do so, but you question the quality of instruction that such a high percentage of part-time instructors can deliver. You believe the reputation of the department is at stake.

All three professors on a search and screening committee in your department are white males, as were the two candidates they recommended. The one minority and one female candidate in the field did receive courtesy interviews, but they did not make the final list that the search committee gave to the chairperson. The chairperson, fearing that the department might have to search again and thus ruin part of the summer vacation, goes along with the recommendations even though he has "doubts." The associate dean is aware that 15 percent of the master's degrees in this particular field have been awarded to women in the last ten years and knows several minority candidates personally. He does not want to go along with the department but is up for evaluation next year by these same individuals. He asks you, a faculty member, to object on his behalf without revealing the source of the objection.

A clever female doctoral candidate is clearly the best choice for a position in your department, but several of your colleagues are threatened by the prospect that she will be employed at the rank of assistant professor and may be promoted to associate professor faster than they will be. They vote against her. You object to this seeming injustice to the candidate, but you feel that if you go to the administration, you might risk your own chances for promotion.

During a departmental search, your colleagues object to the "pushy" behavior of a female candidate while lauding the "aggressiveness" of a male candidate. You, a female member of the department, are afraid to speak out because personnel decisions affecting you are made by your colleagues.

As a new minority faculty member, you have the same obligation to prepare course work and serve on committees as the rest of the faculty. Yet the dean asks you to be the adviser to a large number of minority students because you would "make a good role model." You feel that you are in danger of performing one or more of these responsibilities in a slipshod manner or neglecting your family because of work assignments. You have always wanted to teach at this particular college but are torn between ideals.

Should a college refrain from employing a faculty member who has been previously convicted of a criminal act but has served his time? Should a college admit a student with a criminal record to a program such as criminal justice or accounting?

To punish an "errant" faculty member, a department chairperson assigns her an evening section as part of a teaching schedule that will now stretch from 8 A.M. to 8 P.M. on one day. As a member of the department, you take notice but are reluctant to attract the ire of your chairperson.

You are a member of the collegewide personnel committee. What are the ethical considerations when a department chairperson refuses to recommend the granting of tenure (or a promotion) to an otherwise qualified faculty member because the latter is considered to be outspoken or a rabble-rouser or has in some way offended either the chairperson or a member of the administration?

Without the knowledge of a faculty member, his chairperson places something derogatory in his personnel file. You, a colleague, learn of this from the clerk whose duty it is to put the offensive material in the file.

A faculty member is no longer capable of teaching effectively and, despite having tenure, should be terminated. A senior colleague of yours argues that if the department members allow this termination, they are "paving the way" for their own future removal. The tenured members of the department vote five to four to keep the professor. You are privy to the entire discussion and want to divulge the information to the academic dean. But you would benefit from the senior professor's departure because she is a specialist in your teaching area, and you would get a choice assignment if she were to leave.

You learn that in another department each faculty member has written his or her own evaluation for promotion, each of which has been signed by the department chairperson as her own. However, you and that chairperson have been at odds before, and you would look as if you were trying to get back at her if you reported the activity.

Your committee is investigating this question: Is it ethical to know a problem exists and then take no action? For example, although revelations of sexual or racial harassment may be embarrassing to the college, should the faculty and administration ignore such charges? How should individual rights of the faculty member and student be best protected? How should the college be protected?

You know a faculty member who neglects her primary duties because she is away from the campus too frequently to fulfill other obligations, responsibilities, or just whims. You are proud of her off-campus accomplishments, yet you have been approached by a small student delegation about the quality of on-campus teaching by this departmental colleague.

A faculty member signs a pledge to return to the institution after taking a sabbatical leave. You, a colleague in whom he has confided, know that he does not intend to come back.

A faculty member is using up all of his sick leave but refuses to submit to the institution's requirement that he see its physicians. He says, "Don't you trust me or believe my doctor?" You, his office mate, have good reason to believe he is faking illness.

### Ethical Dilemmas in Governance and Relations Between the College and the Community

A faculty member falsely testifies under oath in an action against the college. You, a colleague, are aware that he is lying. You must decide whether to be loyal to your teaching buddy or to the institution that nurtures you both.

At a cocktail party, you overhear a colleague describing a shady practice of her department. Your colleagues dealt severely with the last whistle-blower. Acceptance by your peers has always been important to you.

You learn from students that a faculty member is "stirring up" the students in her class to speak out against the administration. The president of the student government is in the class, and the faculty member keeps taunting him about student government being a puppet of the administration. Other students in the class complain to you, their faculty adviser.

A small but vocal clique of faculty members levies charges against the president of the college but does not give him time to respond to the charges before they are made public. Because of the furor, a majority of the faculty members may ask for a vote of censure. You know the charges to be untrue, but you are up for promotion and are reluctant to challenge colleagues who have a say over your promotion.

A department chairperson pressures a faculty member to change her vote on some issue crucial to him. You, her office mate, know of the pressure and are caught between your friendship with the colleague and maintaining the integrity of the faculty voice in the deliberative process on the issue.

You, a member of the executive committee of the faculty's union, know that the union has used money from mandatory faculty dues for a nonpermissible expenditure. Is your loyalty to the union higher than your loyalty to the college?

A new trustee knows you, a faculty member, as a neighbor and asks you for your confidential evaluation of the president. You are tempted to use this newfound leverage to achieve your own goals for the institution but are aware of the possible consequences.

The board and the president seek to insulate faculty members from undue political interference, but some of the faculty members invite this interference by criticizing the institution publicly and sending critical statements to the press and legislature. You are tempted to say something critical of this group.

You know a faculty member who has served on an accreditation team at an institution other than his own, has assessed the strengths and weaknesses of that other college, and has applied for a position there. You are called for a reference.

### Ethical Dilemmas in Budget and Finance

You, the chairperson of a department, could provide false and misleading information or withhold important facts so that your budget would go unharmed while another department is put at a disadvantage. You feel that the budget is a zero-sum game; that is, if some other department gets more money, you get less. Yet you have never submitted false information before.

A department chair refuses to split an overly large class section because she is expected to make the department a "cost-effective profit center." As a result, students in this department find themselves in the largest classes on campus and have a high failure rate. You, a senior member of the department, are a friend of the chairperson's but are aware of student complaints.

A donor, about to give a sizable sum of money to your department, disparagingly asks you, the chairperson, if the department caters to any of those "radical" (ethnic, racial, or religious) students. Your department could put the gift to good purpose.

On an approved trip, you find that your expenses are less than you were allotted. You know how difficult it is to get travel money and plan another trip next year for which you might not have such institutional support. Do you pad your bill now and save the additional amount to cover the next trip, or should you return the excess?

A faculty member obtains a grant to publish a book from the foundation of his community college. He fails to list the institution on the book jacket. In fact, he puts down another institution in which he holds an adjunct position because it is more prestigious than the community college. You are his office mate at the community college. Is your friendship with the professor more important than your citizenship with the institution?

### Conclusion

What can one conclude about many of the dilemmas faced almost daily by members of the campus community? One important step is to identify some of the recurring themes and daily ethical challenges faced on most campuses. For example, speaking out on many of the situations in the examples could jeopardize one's professional position or even one's career, especially if the campus climate is not conducive to such dialogue.

Most readers recognize the immediate dilemma posed when one is faced with choosing between the welfare of the individual and

that of the institution. While one hopes that the welfare of the individual and the institution are ultimately one and the same, this is often not apparently the case, especially in the short run. Many of the examples go to the very heart of the debate on what it means to act ethically by asking the reader to solve the dilemma that occurs when personal values conflict with institutional rules, regulations, standards, and expectations.

By noting the common threads running throughout these examples, one realizes that ethical dilemmas will always be a part of campus life. Institutional leaders must send clear signals through their own actions to members of the college community about the kinds of choices they expect them to make and then provide clear channels for addressing and resolving as many of the issues as possible in ethically defensible ways.

Once the institution reaches the stage at which facing and dealing with ethical dilemmas is a part of the institutional culture, leaders will have taken a giant step toward using the tensions resulting from ethical dilemmas in creative ways and will move toward finding solutions that are ethically based and acceptable to members of the college community.

This chapter began with a quote from Omar Bradley accusing us of being nuclear giants and ethical infants. Let it end with a quote of the first-century poet Lucan: "Pygmies placed on the shoulders of giants see more than the giants themselves" (*The Civil War*, Book II, *Didacus Stella*, p. 10).

In this exploration of the many ethical dilemmas faced by community colleges, we should heed the wisdom of both Bradley and Lucan. Our colleges cannot afford brilliance without conscience, cannot afford to be ethical infants. Nor can campus leaders fail to recognize that they are Lucan's pygmies standing on giant moral issues. It is from this perspective that they can identify ethical issues and provide the leadership for dealing with them.

### References

Barr, M. J. "Student Social Concerns." In W. W. May (ed.), *Ethics and Higher Education*. New York: American Council on Education/Macmillan, 1990.

"Boy Scout Without a Compass," *Time,* June 3, 1974, pp. 14–15.

Carnegie Foundation for the Advancement of Teaching. *The Condition of the Professoriate: Attitudes and Trends, 1989.* Princeton, N.J.: Carnegie Foundation for the Advancement of Teaching, 1989.

"College Puts Ethics on Front Burner." *Academic Leader: The Newsletter for Academic Deans and Department Chairs,* 1990, *6*(10), 1.

Gardner, J. *Morale.* New York: W. W. Norton, 1978.

Laney, J. T. "Through Thick and Thin: Two Ways of Talking About the Academy and Moral Responsibility." In W. W. May (ed.), *Ethics and Higher Education.* New York: American Council on Education/Macmillan, 1990.

McCollum, B. "A Pound of Prevention . . . Integration of Ethics into Introductory Accounting." *Innovation Abstracts,* 1990, *12*(23), 2.

May, W. W. (ed.). *Ethics and Higher Education.* New York: American Council on Education/Macmillan, 1990.

Mellert, R. B. "Ethics in Higher Education." *Innovation Abstracts,* 1990, *12*(30), 1–2.

Perlman, D. H. "Ethical Challenges of the College and University Presidency." In W. W. May (ed.), *Ethics and Higher Education.* New York: American Council on Education/Macmillan, 1990.

# Chapter Six

# Business
# and Community
# Linkages

## Karen A. Bowyer

Leaders are people who are reflective, who have gained insights into the human condition, and who make choices that help the rest of us see glimpses of a better society—a society based upon concepts of morality. Reflection upon our relationships to others is extremely important to the furtherance of our moral understandings of society. Thus, how community college leaders can develop a reflective sensitivity to the ethical dimensions of the linkages that must be made when serving a community is the focus of this chapter.

Ethical considerations, as the editor of this book has stated, involve the principles, beliefs, and rules of moral conduct that guide the actions of the members of the college community. To a large extent, the ethical dimensions should be the most important elements of the culture of a college. The primary point that this chapter makes is that the practical relationships between the college, its mission, and the community should be handled in such a way that the integrity of all aspects of the college is maintained.

Ethical dimensions can be as vague, ambiguous, open ended and uncertain as any aspect of the community college agenda. This chapter attempts to clarify in a practical way the ethical dimensions of the connection between the college and business and industry.

## Why Ethics Are a Concern
## in Business and Community Linkages

In the 1970s and 1980s, community colleges created many linkages with universities, public schools, community organizations, businesses, and industries. The 1990s and beyond will likely be a time when existing linkages are expanded and new ones created. Some of these relationships reflect the more traditional roles of the community college, such as providing transfer programs for students who wish to continue their education in four-year colleges or universities. The community college will also continue to offer cooperative, vocational, and technical programs as well as work with high schools to ensure that their graduates are prepared for college study.

The community college extended its traditional mission through offering continuing education programs and various forms of community service. More recently, colleges have established linkages with businesses and industries. Since these linkages place the institution on the edge of the traditional views about education and service, many people have watched closely the emergence of these relationships.

The service mission of the academic world may clash with the for-profit motive of the business world. The basis for any clash will likely be issues of intellectual freedom, ownership, integrity of courses and academic degrees, and ethics. Thus, a discussion of leadership, ethics, and moral foundations seems an appropriate task.

My extensive review of the literature about business and industry linkages with community colleges reveals a deficit in the area of direct discussion of ethical issues. There are some exceptions, of course, such as Powers, Powers, Betz, and Aslanian (1988), Feldman, (1985), Baron (1983), and Stauffer (1983).

Many reasons could be offered for the absence of direct and in-depth analyses of this area. At least three reasons seem relevant here. First, many educational leaders are unaware that they are viewed as moral models by the community. In recent years, the media have devoted more and more attention to college and university personnel who have transgressed the moral standards; that such personnel are viewed as models has been evident in the reporting. Second, considerations of economic benefits may be too powerful for those people who would raise questions about the ethics of a particular linkage. Third, as stated earlier, ethical dimensions are often vague and ambiguous and therefore are troublesome for those people in business and industry as well as those in the community college who are more inclined to be narrowly pragmatic and task oriented.

Certainly it is true that leaders in educational institutions must continue to be sensitive to the general purpose of these institutions—the promotion of learning. This is the guiding ethic for these leaders, the foundation for their treatment of colleagues, students, and the subject matter of teaching. The central virtues of humankind are the traditional ones of goodness, honesty, justice, and truth (Soltis, 1986), and these must be in the forefront of decisions about academic and intellectual freedom, finances, censorship, due process, program integrity, purpose, and mission. These virtues are a part of any serious discussion about ethical dilemmas and practical problems that emerge when a leader attempts to extend the mission of the college through linkages with business and industry while ensuring that the integrity of the institution is maintained and even enhanced.

The community college leader must be especially sensitive to and open about the possibility that ethical concerns may not be uppermost in the thoughts of business and industry leaders and overly entrepreneurial faculty and staff members. Recent events in our economic and social history give substance to such beliefs. The names Boesky, Keating, Trump, and Milkin have certainly been prominent in the news media in connection with the scandals that have enveloped the savings and loans institutions, stock market manipulations, and leveraged buyouts that leave companies strapped with debt. However, throughout all such discussions, the question of moral standards is raised after the facts have been widely broadcast. A number of the people involved in these scandals have freely admitted their guilt, and several are in prison or are soon to be sentenced.

Clearly, in any alliance with business and industry, the community college leader must assert a position of moral leadership before any kind of linkage is established. And if the business or industry response is not appropriately moral and ethical, the college leader must decline or terminate that relationship.

## Types of Linkages

Cooperative relationships between institutions of higher education and business and industrial organizations have been a reality for a great many years. Such linkages increased dramatically in the decades following Sputnik (1957), and much has been written about the nature of these relationships.

Perhaps the most visible relationships are those that involve universities doing scientific research that may have been initiated or strongly supported by the military or by business or industry. This type of cooperation is a natural one in many cases because universities and colleges can provide scientific expertise while businesses and industries can contribute financial aid or state-of-the-art technical support.

Usually, these relationships are beneficial to all concerned and proceed without problems. On occasion, significant problems have arisen when the cooperation revolves around the possible development of a commercial product. For example, research on muscular dystrophy at the University of Tennessee Medical School has proven quite promising for muscular dystrophy patients, and "[o]wnership of a muscle cell transplant technique [Peter] Law developed could be worth millions commercially" (Hamilton, 1990, p.1). The University of Tennesse Research Corporation believes it owns any new techniques that Law developed as a University of Tennessee employee. In this case, conflict will possibly replace cooperation.

The reason for the conflict is quite obvious: the economic gain is potentially enormous and the question of ownership, the researcher's time and salary, the use of university equipment, and any business contributions are dominant issues in the controversy. Moral codes would suggest that the researcher and the university each own part of the invention, but a moral code may not help decide the percentage of ownership of each party. In such cases, the legal system, quite literally, becomes the court of last resort. However, if educational leaders were to assert the moral stance of institutional policies forcefully, many such controversies would never occur and would therefore never be put to the test of legal judgment.

While cooperative arrangements in research play a dominant role in the connection of the university with business and industry, the community college has tended to play a service role. A number of service activities between community colleges and business and industry were reported by the American Council on Education and Business–Higher Education Forum (1984), including support by corporations for college and university programs, support for students, training workshops, conferences, symposia, lectures, recruitment, faculty and student loans, and a variety of joint projects that could fit within the mission of the community college.

### Service Role of Community Colleges

According to James P. Long (1989), in the 1980s, the American Association of Community and Junior Colleges (AACJC) undertook major initiatives with its Putting America Back to Work and Keeping America Working projects. Long writes, "These initiatives provided leadership for a wide range of activities that included: retraining displaced workers, technology transfer, business incubators, partnerships with employers to upgrade employees, high technology centers and parks, and customized training" (1989, p. 161).

Questions about what created this new emphasis for community colleges have been raised by Long and others. A major factor in creating this new emphasis is the change of name from *junior* to *community college* to describe the two-year college. The use of the word *community* is based on a broadened concept of the mission that goes beyond preparation programs for occupations or transfer to a senior institution to that of community service and continuing education. The idea emerged that community colleges were open for all applicants, regardless of age and ethnic background, and that community needs could be met at least partially through college resources.

For whatever reason, community colleges have become a major partner in the development of human beings to their full potential, and a part of that task involves cooperation with business and industry. The rising interest of business and industry in human resource development makes corporate education a growing educational activity in the nation.

Community colleges appear to have an inside track on alliances with business and industry because they are able to respond more rapidly to requests for services than universities can (Parnell, 1982). In addition, community colleges have encouraged adult students, or in the case of business, older workers, to continue their education. As a consequence, college personnel have developed skills and processes for working with these students. This expertise easily translates into productive relationships with businesses and industries, where the older worker is often in need of developmental or remedial education. The open admissions policy of the community college easily accommodates the needs of these learners.

Several authors have suggested a variety of possible activities for the alliances of colleges with businesses and industries (Cross, 1985; Powers, Powers, Betz, and Aslanian, 1988; Deegan and Drisko, 1985). These activities include grants-in-aid, course offerings on the campus or at other locations, cooperative education programs, workshops and short courses, consultative services, joint investment in the hardware of technology, funding of training, contribution of equipment to the college, advisory boards composed of business and industry leaders, jobs for graduates in cooperative businesses, recruitment of new (older, adult) students, and contract training.

Within such relationships lie the possibilities for benefits but also problems that can create serious ethical conflicts. Some of the benefits and problems were noted by Deegan and Drisko (1985), who have written about contract training and the community college based upon their national survey of 1,258 community and two-year technical colleges. They had a 32 percent response rate to their survey (402 colleges), and 69 percent of the respondents (277) had contract training programs (p. 16). From their analysis, the authors were able to identify six benefits as well as six problems that arose from the linkages.

The benefits are improved relationships with business and industry, increased revenue, the opportunity to fulfill the community college mission, increased visibility, the opportunity to provide real-world contact for community college faculty, and beneficial public relations. The problems are lack of qualified instructors, inadequate facilities for training, scheduling of classes around employee work, low internal (college) support, time required for development of courses for contract training, and lack of marketing strategies.

I conducted a limited survey in 1991 to determine if the findings by Deegan and Drisko are still valid in today's community colleges. I also added a dimension that dealt with sensitive issues that might be the source of ethical dilemmas. It seems clear that contract training and similar programs continue to thrive. Respondents mentioned problems such as companies not wanting the regular college faculty to teach the courses because their knowledge was not current, college staff using company data inappropriately, and college staff getting caught between labor and management in the company.

Certainly, any type of relationship has the potential to affect the internal structure and the external functions of the college, and the result can be seen as a benefit or a problem. But it is also possible that the result of the relationship could be a mixture of benefit and problem. At any rate, it is the college, its mission, and its community relations that the administrative leader must be concerned with, for the college cannot monitor the actions of business and industrial personnel. It should be noted that in 1983, 70 percent of U.S. corporations reported that they had well-established written codes of ethics (Stauffer, 1983). Recent actions by many individuals in business would suggest that such codes are ineffective or ignored, a fact that could present problems for community colleges when they contemplate linkages with business and industry.

The crucial question has yet to be asked: What are educational leaders to do when apparently legitimate opportunities and challenges are presented by business and industry leaders? In such cases, the leaders of the college and their colleagues need to consider if there is a single moral standard to which all parties should be required to subscribe. The guiding ethic may come from several sources, such as the mission statement of the college, the history and culture of the institution, and a written code of ethics. To assess the ethical and pragmatic implications of opportunities and challenges, the leader should exhibit a sensitivity for moral deliberation; that is, the leader must recognize that not all parties in a potential cooperative project have the same backgrounds and the same goals.

The leader should ensure that all relevant knowledge is available when the deliberation process begins. The leader must exhibit openness, objectivity, and honesty in the process of considering a proposed action. And the leader must have the courage to assert a position about an action even though the consequences of such a position may be viewed as negative. For example, suppose that an industry wants a college to offer a statistical process control class for college credit to its employees even though the potential students lack the prerequisite skills in mathematics. A request like this will tempt college officials to sacrifice the integrity of their course for potential financial gain. By offering the class, enrollment-driven funding will increase. Moreover, the industry might make a contribution to the college if the college cooperates. The leader of the community college must make the final judgment about the proposed linkage and do so with the full knowledge of the short- and long-range implications for the college (Howe, 1986).

Thus, for community college leaders to consider any of the service activities suggested in the previous pages of this chapter, they and their colleagues must engage in a great deal of reflection. Ethical considerations must come first, and only later should economic and other issues be brought to bear on the situation. The areas of the college most likely to be affected by business and industry linkages are institutional mission and purpose, programs and enrollment, finances and autonomy, faculty, and professional relations. The remaining sections of this chapter offer suggestions for educational leaders as they look for guidance in dealing with dilemmas that necessarily arise in these areas.

## Conflicts over Institutional Mission and Purpose

Marvin J. Feldman (1985) suggests that linkages with business and industry raise some ethical issues, and although these issues are not new, they may have importance for the way the community college views its mission and purpose. Business and industry linkages may well serve as a challenge to institutional identity and the fulfillment of traditional roles.

Such a challenge can come in a variety of ways, but one that seems to create major difficulties is the request for the college to produce materials that are or could be in conflict with its instructional purpose. For example, the research division of an industry may have developed a product that it wishes to market. Suppose that the industry has worked with the college on previous occasions and was impressed with the video-production capability of the college. The industry leaders meet with the college president and suggest that because of the excellent work of the media department, the industry wishes it to develop a videotape that will be used by the industry to market the new product. Of course, the college will receive a generous payment, the media department personnel will receive consultant fees, and credit will come to the college as the industry broadcasts the videotape nationwide.

How will the president of the college react? How should the president react? Where should the president look for guidance? To add a small complication, the media department needs new equipment to provide instructional materials for regular classes, and the industry payment would be a substantial contribution toward its purchase. Other college funds are not available. In addition, the new product is one that will decrease pollutants and is environmentally safe. Of course, by producing the videotape, the college could possibly take work away from a local business.

Weighing the pros and cons would not be a sufficient response to the ethical questions raised by this dilemma. The discussion of the situation should certainly include the positive elements to be gained by the college, especially the future production capability of the media department. The president and his or her colleagues should look to the mission statement of the college. Perhaps this request conflicts with the purpose of the video department, which may be to produce instructional materials. If the president does accept the project, has the mission of the college been subverted? Has the college deserted its moral stance on intellectual and academic freedom? Will the college have full control over the message of the videotape? Has the profit motive overruled concepts of truth, honesty, and fairness?

Some help in such a situation may come from the Educational Business Activities Policy Statement of the AACJC, which says that each educational business activity should meet the following five conditions:

1. The activity is deemed to be an integral part in the fulfillment of the institution's teaching and public service mission and other educational support activities without regard to surplus revenue;

2. The activity is needed to provide an integral good or service at a reasonable price, on reasonable terms, and at a convenient location and time;

3. The activity is carried out for the primary benefit of the campus community but with sensitivity to the whole community;

4. The college must comply with applicable laws and regulations pertaining to such activities, and educational business activities not falling within the guidelines established above may be unrelated business income activities;

5. The college should consult with employer advisory committees on any occupational education program whereby it is necessary for the college to operate a business in conjunction with the training program [American Association of Community and Junior Colleges, 1991, p. 169].

In their analysis of policy issues and the future, Deegan and Drisko (1985) suggest that community college personnel consider a series of policy questions if the college is thinking about beginning or expanding contract training. Although the questions refer to contract training, they clearly have significance for other business and industry linkages.

Two of the questions are pertinent for this discussion. First, what will be the place and priority of contract training programs in the mission of the college? And second, what impact will the programs have on institutional values and reward systems?

The college leader must think seriously about and devote much time to the possible answers to these questions because ethical issues can arise from both the benefits and the problems of cooperative projects. For example, whether tax-supported institutions should be available to businesses and industries so that they do not have to provide their own training division and thereby employ a training staff is a critical issue (Long, 1989). The broader question is whether the college is an extension of the for-profit business world or whether an extension program is a legitimate college service and in the best interests of all taxpayers.

The college leader must review all requests for training and other types of service and ask whether the request fits within the instructional mission of the college or the extension or public service mission of the college. Without this careful review, it is possible that the college would end up providing low-cost training that may not be in the best interests of the college and ultimately the taxpayer (Tillery and Deegan, 1985).

The state of Virginia, where resources are very limited, is considering a recommendation that businesses pay higher tuition fees than regular students for their employees (Barmettler, 1990). Limited class sections in community colleges are usually filled by students seeking degrees and employees in business and industry. Those students who for economic reasons may wait to register until the last minute are thus eliminated. Often, these are part-time and high-risk students who could become more productive with additional education. It might be in the national interest to provide state-subsidized education to these economically disadvantaged students and to ask that businesses and industries pay the full cost of education for their employees.

A word of caution for the college that does not have but is considering the development of linkages with business and industry: the leaders of the college should devote a great deal of time to articulating institutional mission and purpose before entering into a series of relationships that might have an impact upon the traditional role of the college. Of course, it is possible to enter such relationships with the purpose of changing the institutional mission (Teitel, 1988).

Those institutions that already have contracts of various kinds should set a specific schedule for continual review of institutional mission. The independence and sense of identity of the college can be lost through relationships with business and industry, particularly if the relationships provide resources that are sorely needed to continue offering traditional educational experiences for students. However, the very people for whom the resources were intended may not receive them because they have been crowded out of the educational arena by the business relationship. Energy, time, and commitment to traditional offerings may have diminished so gradually that only the students (or those who had hoped to be students) are aware of the loss. The subtleties of dependence will often blur the clarity of thinking of those who have responsibility for maintaining an appropriate college mission.

## Conflicts over Programs and Enrollment

Deegan and Drisko (1985) suggest that additional opportunities for curriculum development, along with several other benefits, are positive results that can accrue when a college undertakes contract training. Certainly, program development might be enhanced since the opportunity for community colleges to work with personnel from business and industry may bring a new sense of real-world experience to the curriculum.

However, businesses and industries may request credit courses or even parallel programs that are geared at a different and in many cases lower level than the regular program. Often such a request is accompanied by an offer that the courses be located onsite and that some or all aspects of the courses be taught by personnel other than regular, full-time faculty members of the college.

In this case, the president must consider whether the college is being asked to legitimize a less than acceptable course or program. Will fulfilling this request lead to an attack upon the integrity of other courses and programs of the college? Will a decision to offer on-site courses mean that the industry, not the college, retains control over course content? Is this request a subtle attempt to indoctrinate those students enrolled in the course rather than offer them the opportunity to think clearly about the issues? The issues of intellectual honesty and truth must certainly be in the minds of those who must make the decision about entering such an arrangement.

A threat to admission standards set by the professionals within the college or in the larger system of higher education may also be embedded in such a request. These standards represent the best judgment of academic leaders about levels of achievement and sound academic learning. When faced with such requests, the community college leader must consider the integrity of programs within the college. One such attempt to maintain integrity comes from the state of Tennessee.

A technical certificate of credit was developed in the community colleges of Tennessee when it became clear that the academic certificate of credit did not meet the training needs of employers. Students taking courses for technical certificates are classified as nondegree students, while students enrolling in courses designed for academic certificates are subject to all the requirements of regular admission. Academic certificate students must have basic skills at the twelfth grade level before entering college-level work. Technical certificate students may enter technical training without having their basic skills assessed.

Although these two credentials help maintain the integrity of the academic certificate, the colleges in Tennessee still have problems in meeting the training needs of business and industry without lowering standards. For example, in a limited survey, I found that some industrial employees taking statistical process control classes in Tennessee community colleges do not have the prerequisite skills in mathematics. The instructor is thus forced to teach the course at a lower level than normal to meet the needs of these students.

Many institutions avoid this ethical dilemma by offering continuing education courses for business and industry. Since continuing education courses are usually self-supporting and not funded by state formulas, they are not as financially attractive to college leaders as credit courses. Therefore, colleges are tempted to offer these courses for credit in order to receive the state funding in addition to the fees from the students.

Paul Elsner, chancellor of Maricopa Community College District, must have been thinking about this situation when he and his staff considered the massive enrollment increase due to special training offered the 12,000 employees at a new Motorola plant in Phoenix, Arizona. At a regional workshop sponsored by the Presidents Academy of the American Association of Community and Junior Colleges in Santa Fe, New Mexico, on June 7, 1990, Elsner told the assembled group that the full-time enrollment from the Motorola training was not counted for regular formula funding since it was too short lived. He also said that the enrollment in courses offered by corporate services at Maricopa Community College had the potential of becoming larger than the regular enrollment. He, along with others, speculates about how much community colleges should do for the corporate sector.

It seems clear that a college must maintain its perspective (or balance) in the areas of liberal arts and general education and in the vocational and technical programs that have been associated with the college for some time. As Feldman (1985) states, "There is a danger that we will build a society in which everybody knows how to make a good living and nobody knows how to live a good life" (p. 191). He notes that the vocational educators are often the advocates for including liberal arts courses in degree programs. But in most training programs, general education and liberal arts courses are excluded because businesses and industries are not inclined to pay for learning they do not consider to be related to the job.

If businesses and industries want their employees to earn an associate degree, college leaders must insist that general education and liberal arts be part of that degree. If college leaders insist on this condition, they would do much to offset the criticism that customized contract training programs may sound the death knell for liberal arts in community colleges (Pincus, 1985). Experience suggests, however, that general education and liberal arts will remain a strong part of the community college.

Often, programs such as liberal arts may be maintained with the extra compensation gained through contracts with business and industry. But the college must deal with the question of whether the means justify the ends; that is, will the long-range ethical position of the college be undermined by short-range decisions that seem to be justifiable?

Those people in leadership positions in community colleges are the gatekeepers for the integrity of community college credit courses. If they give college credits away, they may have trouble convincing the public that they offer a high-quality education. It would be good to follow the advice of Robert McCabe (1985, p. 94), who says, "College credits must be viewed as currency, and institutions must not award credits until course standards have been met."

## Conflicts over Finances and Autonomy

Publicly supported institutions of higher education have suffered in recent years in a variety of ways. The reform movement in education in this country has had a great influence on the way the public perceives education at all levels. Tax-paying citizens become distressed when they read and hear about students graduating from high school without the skills of reading, writing, and calculating. They are even more distressed when they learn about the remedial and developmental programs that have become a significant part of college and university offerings. The result is predictable—no support for budget increases, no support for tax increases for education, and, in some cases, proposed cuts in budgets, especially in a climate of economic downturn. Some higher education institutions are experiencing enrollment declines, thus causing loss of tuition. Others are experiencing enrollment increases, thus causing the institution to stretch its existing resources.

The finances of a college can be improved in several ways through the business and industry connection. By offering workshops, seminars, and college credit courses, a college enlarges its enrollment base and may receive increased funding from the state and local funding agencies based upon student enrollment in credit courses. Sometimes, businesses and industries will provide gifts of equipment, money, and even personnel to support some aspect of a college program.

The leaders of the college should give thought to the possibility of such gifts prior to entering into the relationship. Outright gifts to the college from a business or industry must be just that—they must not have stipulations or restrictions attached or intended. The president must make it clear to the donor that the integrity of the college and its autonomy will not be compromised. Certainly, from a moral position and even more so from a legal one, the college administration must certify that all money derived from the business linkage is used in a manner that is open to inspection from auditors and any other public official. Any deviation from these ethical and legal principles can spell disaster for the future of extended services at the college.

When a contract is negotiated between a business and a college, several issues that can prove to be crucial may not be obvious to the inexperienced administrator. For example, whether the intended course, workshop, or seminar is to be offered at the college or on-site can prove to be critical because the question of control may become cloudy. Although this issue has been mentioned before, it bears repeating because it is such an important element in maintaining the integrity of programs and the autonomy of the institution.

If a course, workshop, or seminar is to be held on-site, the college may have difficulty monitoring the teaching and faculty, possibly because of a lack of personnel. The business could reschedule the class, or it may decide to hold some other function during the time a class is scheduled and not inform college officials. Moreover, on-site offerings may be subject to subtle control because a business is biased about sensitive issues such as pollution, smoking, or chemical waste. The business may attempt to abridge the academic freedom of a faculty member of the college. For example, a company that is discharging excessive chemical wastes into the local rivers and streams may not want the instructor of a course in safety and health to discuss the health hazards to the community from such actions. Or a meat packing plant may not want the community college literature class to read and discuss Upton Sinclair's *The Jungle*. Such efforts would reveal the business's motive of control and profit and certainly would constitute a form of censorship. These and other actions would subvert the instructional mission of the college, which is, in part, to liberate the individual through providing broad, uncensored educational experiences.

One must recognize the basic differences that exist between the business world and the educational institution. The college leader must certainly keep the institution financially sound. The business world's profit, some of which accrues to the college, can be the source of much needed support for the college budget. Perhaps profit for the college is in disseminating some aspect of education to an as yet unserved group. Thus the college helps fulfill its mission of educating the citizenry of the community.

Some colleges tend to be slow to respond to requests for help in training. Businesses and industries have a difficult time understanding this slow pace, but it stems from the nature of the bureaucracy of higher education. Community colleges, however, are able to respond more rapidly than universities. Business leaders want a quick response and may become impatient with a college. The college leader must resist all efforts that would subvert the thoughtful consideration of requests. If the leader responds too quickly and without due consideration, he or she may be deserting the heritage of rationality of the college (Useem, 1986).

Community colleges must consider the total community and not just the needs of one segment or another such as community leaders, politicians, minorities, or business and industry. This is especially the case when the chamber of commerce is courting a prospective client who may set up a business that will hire many local citizens. For example, the business or industry may insist that the college set up a laboratory for a particular kind of manufacturing systems technology that may be useful only for that industry. Even though the industry will donate all of the technology, the college leader must carefully examine the practical and ethical issues related to autonomy, control, and long-term effect. In a relatively short span of time, the profit outlook for the industry might be severely diminished, and the business may cease operation or may be acquired by another company that is not interested in continuing the relationship with the college. The college may be left with a vast amount of hardware that takes up valuable space and that has little or no relationship to the instructional program. In addition, this linkage may have alienated other segments of the community, both internal and external to the college. In the process of attracting new industry, college officials must be careful not to promise more than they can deliver.

The college leader must be especially sensitive to the independence of the college and must avoid the possibility that the college is dependent upon contracts with other sectors. This caution includes federally funded programs, for like support from a business, support from the government could be terminated at any time. Financial support should be a secondary consideration in linkages with other sectors because it gives a short-term gain. The honesty and integrity of personnel and programs must be uppermost in the minds of the decision makers who set directions for the future of a great many other individuals.

### Conflicts over Faculty Members

Full-time faculty members who teach in contract training programs can be a positive force in the community and can make different sectors of the community aware of the competence of personnel at the college. Yet when the college commits itself to fulfilling contracts with business and industry, it may not have enough full-time faculty members to meet the teaching demands. The use of part-time and adjunct faculty members in these training programs can be a source of grave concern.

This was the case in the award-winning program of Hazard Community College (HCC) in Kentucky and the Hazard-Perry Chamber of Commerce. The Business and Industry Technical Assistance Center (BITAC) at Hazard Community College was founded in 1986 and was originally designed to use the full-time business faculty of the school to help solve the community's problem of high unemployment. But as the activities of the center increased, the availability of full-time faculty members decreased to the point at which almost all of the classes for BITAC were taught by adjunct faculty members.

To remedy this situation, the BITAC semester was instituted. During this semester, a faculty member is released from a portion of his or her teaching responsibilities to serve as a BITAC resource person. Faculty members from various disciplines are encouraged to participate if they have a skill that would benefit the clients of BITAC.

The college envisioned the following five benefits of such an arrangement:

1.  Gain a rotating liaison between the faculty and BITAC
2.  Give faculty members with specific skills needed in the community an opportunity to offer those skills on an extended basis
3.  Enable BITAC to plan better for faculty participation and to make better use of the resources of the college
4.  Enable faculty members to enjoy a learning experience through the BITAC semester that will result in more specific applications of theory and more practical classroom outcomes benefiting both faculty and students
5.  Enable BITAC to serve the business community better

The example shows how large numbers of full-time faculty members can be involved in contract training. The reasons for using adjunct faculty members in these programs are many, but the five benefits cited above should encourage a college to overcome the many obstacles to using full-time faculty members.

### Conflicts over Professional Relations

When one writes or speaks of professional relations, the implication is that the linkages between the college and business and industry are mutually beneficial. However, the meaning of the word *professional* may vary considerably in the world of business and industry from the meaning of that term in the community college, even though both groups will claim to be professional in their dealings with clients.

For the educator, to be professional means having respect for others' rights, responsibilities, opinions, and humanity. In addition, the professional in education must be objective about beliefs, must not be authoritarian, and must participate as an equal in reaching a decision about an issue. For the professional educator, the integrity of the teaching and learning process must remain at the top of the list of professional attributes.

For the business professional, the focus must necessarily be different. Without a doubt, the profit motive, which must be dominant in the mission of business, will significantly influence the decision-making process of business professionals. In all probability, decision making will be more authoritarian in nature, and objectivity about product will probably not be at the top of the list, thus creating a difficult ethical dimension to the relationship with the college.

## Conclusion

Most interpreters of the linkage between business and industry and the community college seem to agree that the benefits from such relationships far outweigh the drawbacks. There is little doubt that colleges will continue to seek linkages of various sorts with a variety of external institutions. From the viewpoint of the college, these relationships occur in the arena of economic and human resource development. Both arenas are of vast significance in a democratic political system and in a capitalistic economic system. The glue that should hold these systems together is a code of ethics upon which decisions about values, morality, fairness, right, wrong, honesty, truth, and good can be based.

Any approach to ethics should be based in pragmatics, for the theoretical approach to ethics is not what is called for here. The guiding ethic must deal with factual data, must be reflective (rational), must be based on knowledge of alternatives, and must have insights into another's background of experiences. To act responsibly using the guiding ethic requires a great deal of courage.

Perhaps more than anything else, ethics must serve as the guiding principle for those who are engaged in (or may wish to engage in) extended service to business and industry. Short-range gains must be placed into the perspective of the long-range mission of the college. The choices that face college leaders must be evaluated from the perspective of mission, integrity, and autonomy for the institution. To evaluate them otherwise may lead to a sacrifice of the future for the institution and all those who are a part of it.

## References

American Association of Community and Junior Colleges. *AACJC Membership Directory, 1991.* Washington, D.C.: American Association of Community and Junior Colleges, 1991.

American Council on Education and Business–Higher Education Forum. *Corporate and Campus Cooperation: An Action Agenda.* Washington, D.C.: American Council on Education and Business–Higher Education Forum, 1984.

Barmettler, B. "Service Demands Up and Resources Down." *Richmond Times-Dispatch,* Nov. 4, 1990.

Baron, R. "Higher Education and the Corporate Sector: Ethical Dilemmas." In M. Baca and R. H. Stein (eds.), *Ethical Principles, Practices, and Problems in Higher Education.* Springfield, Ill.: Thomas, 1983.

Cross, K. P. "Determining Missions and Priorities for the Fifth Generation." In W. L. Deegan, D. Tillery, and Associates, *Renewing the American Community College: Priorities and Strategies for Effective Leadership.* San Francisco: Jossey-Bass, 1985.

Deegan, W. L., and Drisko, R. "Contract Training in Community Colleges." *Community and Junior College Journal,* 1985, 55(6), 14–17.

Feldman, M. J. "Establishing Linkages with Other Educational Providers." In W. L. Deegan, D. Tillery, and Associates, *Renewing the American Community College: Priorities and Strategies for Effective Leadership.* San Francisco: Jossey-Bass, 1985.

Hamilton, J. "Researcher Crippled Fund Offer with UT." *Memphis Commercial Appeal,* Nov. 21, 1990.

Howe, K. R. "A Conceptual Basis for Ethics in Teacher Education." *Journal of Teacher Education,* 1986, 37(3), 5–12.

Long, J. P. "The College/Private Sector Connection." In T. O'Banion (ed.), *Innovation in the Community College.* New York: Macmillan, 1989.

McCabe, R. H. "Equity and Quality in College Education: An Essential American Priority." In J. B. Bennett and J. W. Peltason (eds.), *Contemporary Issues in Higher Education: Self-Regulation and the Ethical Roles of the Academy.* New York: American Council on Education/Macmillan, 1985.

Parnell, D. "Putting America Back to Work: Community, Technical, Junior Colleges Ready." *Community and Junior College Journal,* 1982, *52,* 12–15.

Pincus, F. L. "Customized Contract Training in Community Colleges: Who Really Benefits?" Paper presented at a meeting of the American Sociological Association, Washington, D.C., 1985.

Powers, D. R., Powers, M. F., Betz, F., and Aslanian, C. B. *Higher Education in Partnership with Industry: Opportunities and Strategies for Training, Research, and Economic Development.* San Francisco: Jossey-Bass, 1988.

Soltis, J. F. "Teaching Professional Ethics." *Journal of Teacher Education,* 1986, *37*(3), 2–4.

Stauffer, T. M. "Ethics of Cross-Sector Cooperation—The Case of Business and Higher Education." In M. Baca and R. H. Stein (eds.), *Ethical Principles, Practices, and Problems in Higher Education.* Springfield, Ill.: Thomas, 1983.

Teitel, L. "The Impact of Business and Industry Oriented Programs on Community Colleges." Unpublished doctoral dissertation, Graduate School of Education, Harvard University, 1988.

Tillery, D., and Deegan, W. L. "The Evolution of Two-Year Colleges Through Four Generations." In W. L. Deegan, D. Tillery, and Associates, *Renewing the American Community College: Priorities and Strategies for Effective Leadership.* San Francisco: Jossey-Bass, 1985.

Useem, E. L. *Low Tech Education in a High Tech World: Corporations and Classrooms in the New Information Society.* New York: Free Press, 1986.

# Chapter Seven

# Trustees and Governing Boards

## Gary W. Davis

The governing board plays a crucial role in setting the moral tone of a college. The values of the board affect institutional behaviors and the choices of the college faculty and staff members and students. Although most behavior by board members is exemplary, any lapse in board ethics is disturbing. For example, the way board members are selected can generate concern. Are trustees sometimes appointed merely to fulfill a political promise? Do trustees serve only to profit politically and financially, or are they prepared to make the personal sacrifices that ethical trusteeship entails?

If reports are to be believed, some trustees have engaged in all types of unethical behavior. Some have hidden business relationships with companies that hold contracts with the college that their board governs. Other trustees have worked for or been paid by colleges they govern. Some have sold goods and services to their college or encouraged it to do business with close friends or relatives. A few reportedly have participated in board decisions about hiring their relatives or friends. A few have been accused of submitting false or inappropriate expense claims for travel or of telling the president

146

to do the same. Some trustees have made private agreements with their board colleagues that were then translated into official action at board meetings. Others have played detective in an effort to gather evidence against another board member, the college president, or another college employee and then manipulated the press for their own advantage at the expense of the other member of the college community. Out of personal pique, some have worked to blacklist terminated presidents and administrative officers. Others have leaked confidential information to the press or to unions.

Accounts of questionable behavior by trustees and governing boards make board ethics a vital topic for both trustees and presidents. Each occasion of unethical behavior by trustees and boards weakens the moral fiber of the college community. Faculty and staff members as well as students are less likely to put the good of the college above personal benefit if they see board members setting irresponsible examples. The converse is also true; if trustees steadfastly refuse to use their office for personal gain, other members of the college community will be inclined to set high moral standards for themselves.

How can responsible, ethical behavior by boards and trustees be encouraged? Should discussions with trustees focus on the values of the board members or the values of the board as a whole? How can trustees learn to recognize and address ethical issues? What occasions present ethical challenges to governing board members? Can policy making help the board meet its ethical responsibility? What can boards do when they face ethical dilemmas? How should boards and trustees react to unethical practices by a member of their own board or a member of another board within their system? These are the questions to be addressed in this chapter.

## Misconceptions About Ethics

Trustees ought to act on behalf of their fellow citizens when they govern a college. Society trusts the board members to be responsible for an institution that serves the common good. To maintain that trust, governing board members should be willing to put aside personal interest and act instead to protect society by protecting the college. Each trustee ought to be able to say no to offers that would bring personal benefit at the expense of the governed institution.

How can trustees identify and properly resolve ethical issues? They might begin by recognizing some myths about morality and ethics. Perhaps the most common misconception is the notion that ethics is "easy" and morality is "hard." According to this mistaken view, everyone knows what constitutes good behavior, but few people can bring themselves to act in this way. But in complex situations, what constitutes good behavior is not obvious. Ethics, then, is largely a matter of developing a clear understanding of the issues and alternatives that each situation presents.

Unfortunately, a clear perception of the good is often obscured by misconceptions. It is best to begin by saying what ethical behavior is not. It is not merely a matter of style or personal preference. The idea that right can be whatever we want it to be or whatever society dictates is unfortunately all too common. This misconception results from a modern tolerance of many different value systems. In the United States and other so-called secular societies, a number of cultural subgroups and ethical orientations are legally allowed. Toleration of multiple value systems, however, does not make each system equally valid. This toleration allows each person and group the freedom to advocate a set of values and to challenge the prevailing value systems of society. Boards must allow challenges to their ethics, but they are not obligated to abandon their convictions in the face of such challenges.

The good cannot be defined without reference to facts, evidence, and logic. Careful attention to facts can help resolve ethical dilemmas. A debate about the ethics of spending college dollars on travel by board members, for example, might be averted through an examination of the activities in question. When board members attend a seminar to gain information needed in their role as trustees, the activity in question deserves to be described as trustee training rather than travel. Improperly identified activities and issues can easily give rise to misunderstanding and unwarranted conclusions. Any good discussion of ethics begins with a thorough discussion of the facts. Such a discussion may not always remove the need for debate, but at least it puts any ensuing debate on solid, factual ground.

Ethical behavior is not inherently impractical—ethics can be useful. Discussions of right and wrong, if properly focused and moderated, can help both parties in a dispute see the issue from the other's point of view. Understanding the opponent's position on an issue is the first step in finding a solution to the conflict that is acceptable to both sides.

Ethical sensitivity can help board members develop negotiating skills that will be useful when the board's relationships with branches of government, sister institutions, unions, and other groups become adversarial. By leading people toward a common understanding and a shared set of values, ethics can become the glue that binds members of a society (or a board) together. When members of a group know that they share some values with one another and perhaps disagree on others, they can better anticipate each other's positions. Mutual understanding can become the basis for a growing trust. In other words, a shared set of values strengthens the cohesiveness of a group or a society.

On the other hand, ethical behavior is not always practical. Although some people believe that ethics can be counted on to encourage social cooperation and compliance, ethical considerations often disrupt the social process. Because they challenge commonly accepted wisdom and authority, prophets and critics are viewed as a danger to society and its objectives. Ethically motivated campaigns such as the civil rights movement often create social disruption in their wake. People pursue such movements and concerns not for their social benefit but because the movements and concerns are right. Trustees would search in vain for a practical justification for every example of ethical behavior by the board. In many cases, the practical justification simply does not exist.

Ethical behavior does not automatically result from pure motives and intentions. A famous utopian experiment in America failed when the participants spent so much time examining and purifying their motives that they forgot to plant the seeds that would have provided a crop to support the community. An obsession with one's intentions to the exclusion of action is tantamount to ethical default. Right action requires more than pure motives.

The good is not merely a product of responsible behavior by individuals. In human affairs, the good comes about only when individuals act responsibly and when they find effective ways to interact with one another. Responsibility, in other words, has both individual and corporate dimensions. It is not hard to imagine a group of seven or eight trustees, each acting in a manner he or she believes is ethical, failing to reach sound decisions as a board. For trustees to act responsibly, they must be able to reach ethical decisions collectively. When he or she is part of a board that cannot make decisions, a single trustee lacks ethical impact.

## The Role of Value Systems

With myths about ethics debunked, trustees can proceed to examine how sound ethical judgments may be made. Decisions are shaped by the nature of one's value system. Most people adopt a series of value systems during their lifetime. In their first stage of moral development, human beings value pleasure and resist pain. At the next stage, individuals begin to value pride through adherence to rules or through loyalty to a group.

For many people, rule keeping or loyalty represents the highest stage of moral achievement. However, some people feel that even cherished beliefs and groups should sometimes be sacrificed to bring about the best result for the greatest number of people. Still others advocate adherence to universal ethical principles that benefit all humanity. For them, even the greatest good for the greatest number of people is undesirable if it creates an injustice for some other person or group.

The members of a board may have a number of different value systems. The variety of ethical frameworks to be found within a typical community college board results, in part, from the rich diversity of its members' ethnic, economic, and social backgrounds. Because their values and methods for making responsible decisions differ, reasonable trustees occasionally disagree about ethical issues. Such disagreements are to be expected and can be resolved amicably when trustees use orientation sessions, board evaluations, retreats, and so on, to learn more about each other's values and methods for making ethical judgments.

A person's moral sensitivity on a given issue varies according to his or her value system and appreciation of other ethical frameworks. For example, a board member who beliefs that loyalty is the highest good may suggest concealing a failure of the college. Unless the other board members appreciate their colleague's stage of moral development, they may mistakenly classify his views as unethical rather than as an expression of institutional loyalty.

### Values of the Responsible Life

Sensitivity to others' ethical frameworks is the first step in responsible decision making. A second step for a board is to reach consensus on a set of shared values. As a starting point, several commonly held values are listed below. Some originated from the teaching of Michael Josephson of the Joseph and Edna Josephson Institute in Marina del Rey, California.

### *Legality*

Although there is more to ethical behavior than obeying the law, the responsible trustee recognizes that social institutions and their guardians are indebted to the rule of law for their structure and security. Upon taking office, many trustees are required to swear an oath of loyalty to the government and the Constitution. Whether or not trustees take such an oath, the college's debt to society and its laws is beyond dispute. Only the law-abiding college and its trustees can expect to enjoy continued support of society.

Service on a board imposes new legal requirements on a trustee. For example, in many states trustees are required to decline compensation by the college they serve and avoid commercial transactions with the college. A new member of a board should ask the board chair and the college president to summarize the legal obligations of a trustee and the board. In responding to such requests, the president may wish to ask the institution's attorney for assistance. Regular legal updates of board members are also a good idea. The old maxim is right—ignorance of the law is no excuse.

### *Equity*

*Equity* is another word for *fairness*. Trustees are expected not to play favorites. Unfortunately, inequitable treatment of others is often inadvertent. Rather than intending to be unfair, the board may simply forget how it treated similar cases in the past. Consequently, the judgments of the board can take on a random character that many people take to be favoritism. Whether intended or not, inequitable treatment erodes confidence and trust in the decision maker.

Through careful policy making, a board can avoid unfair decisions. Policies are simply guidelines on how, in general, similar situations should be treated. Unfortunately, many board members resist writing down policies in the mistaken belief that written policies do not permit flexibility. In reality, well-written policies permit flexibility when circumstances justify an exception to the general rule.

### Honesty and Openness

Some trustees believe that being completely open is the only acceptable way to be honest. Unfortunately, complete openness is not always allowed by law or the dictates of loyalty. If honesty is defined as trustworthiness rather than as unrestrained openness, a trustee can be honest while preserving the values of loyalty, caring, and respect for the law.

Although disclosure may be inappropriate in certain prescribed circumstances, the habit of telling the truth is right and tends to build trust of the board members by district residents and members of the college community. Ethically mature trustees agree to keep confidences and to preserve an orderly and consistent flow of information through the president and board chairperson, but they are also forthright and trustworthy in their statements and insistent that the board conduct its business in public. Within the limits of discretion, ethical trustees also should be frank with the president and other members of the board. Trustees ignore the value of honesty when they make secret agreements with the president or with other board members. Such private agreements destroy the trust that is required for board teamwork.

### Integrity

Honesty contributes to one's reputation for integrity. Integrity characterizes the trustee whose behavior is free of contradictions. People of integrity consistently act in conformity with a unified vision of themselves. They have a firm grasp of their beliefs, values, and role. As a logical extension of those beliefs and values, their behavior is integrated (of one piece).

A trustee's integrity is violated when the trustee tries to fulfill two incompatible roles. Unfortunately, conflicts of interest can result from a board member's attempt to be helpful or loyal. A board member who, because of loyalty to a political party, opposes a college affirmative action plan or agrees to supply the colleges with goods and services at a price below cost becomes not only a board member but a political party agent or a vendor. Such dual roles are the essence of a conflict of interest, and often the person caught in the conflict is the last one to sense that there is a problem. Conflicts of interest are one of the greatest dangers to a trustee's integrity. They could be avoided if trustees asked themselves, Could I be perceived in this action to be filling two incompatible roles when I ought to be filling one, that of a guardian of the college?

Threats to integrity also arise when a trustee's arguments are rejected by the board. Conventional wisdom holds that the trustee must then support the decision of the board. But what if the trustee continues to feel that the board is wrong and that the college will suffer because a bad decision has been made? The wise trustee must simply admit that both loyalty (to be discussed below) and integrity are important and that sometimes one must be sacrificed for the sake of the other. The trustee must consider the question, What will create the greater harm, support of the board's decision or my failure to support it?

### Fidelity

The value of fidelity is closely related to integrity and characterizes people who keep their promises. Promise keeping enables society to function smoothly by building trust among its members. Without trust, commercial as well as social transactions would be impossible. When promises are broken, cynicism replaces trust, and human beings withdraw into themselves. Cooperation and teamwork vanish. Unfortunately, our strong attachment to openness and individualism in this country tends to undercut trust and fidelity. Some people believe that because an increasing number of trustees reached adulthood during the iconoclastic 1960s, the values of fidelity and promise keeping are not as common in boardrooms as they once were.

### Loyalty

Loyal people respect and obey the decisions of the group to which they belong. Loyalty is a source of group-oriented behavior and challenges the individual trustee to defend the interests of his or her group or groups. Community college trustees should demonstrate loyalty to the college, its customs, and its officers and especially to the board on which they serve.

Although they also may act out of respect for their nation, state, or political constituency, board members should remember that their primary loyalty should be to the board and its decisions, whether or not they originally supported those decisions. Upon joining the board, trustees ought to trade their old allegiances to limited special interests (such as a political party, a faculty union, or a taxpayers group) for a new, primary loyalty to the board and its college. To do anything else would be to default on the responsibility to build the board that no other person or group is in a position to assume.

Whenever disloyalty weakens a board, the college that depends on its leadership suffers the consequences. Only through loyalty to the board can trustees give the college the support it deserves. Much of the reported unethical behavior by boards results from decisions of a trustee to assume power and authority that should be reserved for the board as a whole. Disloyalty also can be expressed by a member's lack of attention to board business. When a trustee's competing loyalties create tardiness or uninformed involvement, the time has come for the trustee to resign.

### Courtesy and Respect

As their concept of loyalty deepens, trustees develop a capacity for understanding customs, traditions, and beliefs unlike their own. Courtesy and respect are values cherished by those who recognize the right of others to be different. Rather than enforcing conformity upon those around them, respectful trustees try to hear and understand varying points of view. To do so, they listen carefully and show respect for others. For example, they arrive for board meetings on time, pay close attention to board proceedings, and stay until adjournment. Because they listen to others does not mean that they have no convictions of their own. To the contrary, listening helps board members defend their opinions and values.

### Caring

Courtesy signals caring. A caring trustee identifies with the plight and needs of others. Rejecting callousness, complacency, and self-centeredness, the caring trustee looks for appropriate ways to serve others. Although caring trustees cannot always use their position on a board to help everyone in need, they do not hesitate to express concern for others and their hope that the college will appropriately serve the needs of the district.

Unfortunately, some trustees use radical forms of self-denial to demonstrate their caring nature. For example, to show concern over others' needs, some boards refuse to invest college funds in trustee development. Such behavior is roughly equivalent to physicians' passing up refresher courses in order to lower fees for their patients. To guard their patients' welfare, truly caring doctors would attend first to their own educational needs. The analogy points to the need to balance concerns. Caring should be informed by wisdom and not used as a political ploy or as a tool for self-aggrandizement.

Caring requires time and energy. Often the sacrifices trustees make affect the trustees' families and friends and reflect their caring as well. A board member who cares is willing to give up personal pleasures (including family and recreational time) to study board issues and to attend board meetings, training sessions for trustees, and college events. Colleges are wise to recognize the dedication of trustees and to thank them both publicly and privately for their faithful service. Whenever possible, colleges also should recognize the sacrifices of families and find appropriate ways to thank them for making faithful service possible.

## Excellence

Responsible people strive for excellence in all they do. And they expect others to perform at the highest levels of their ability. A trustee's performance can be an inspiration to the governing board and college or it can be a signal that little will be given and little expected of others. The opposite of excellence is not only shoddiness but also mediocrity. Because mediocrity is generally not threatening, it produces no anxiety in others. It requires a minimum of energy and imagination and is the natural product of apathy and complacency.

Society traditionally expects its schools and colleges to be bastions of excellence, to identify and transmit the highest human achievements. A trustee who fails to recognize the college's passion for excellence will not be able to understand the faculty and staff members of the institution. College students, faculty members, and staff members are dedicated to teaching and learning the very best of human achievement. Among colleges and college communities, competition and pride in discovery are very important. College employees expect trustees to display a similar passion for excellence in their roles as board members. As ethical trustees, they are obligated to do so.

## Accountability

Their frequent reports to students and to those who channel resources to institutions show that colleges are excellent stewards. Recently, colleges have mastered new ways to report their problems and successes to the public. In the last few years, the public has become interested in accountability and, increasingly, is learning more about institutions of higher learning. However, the new emphasis on accountability has offended some professors, college administrators, and trustees. They believe that academic freedom is abridged whenever colleges are required to report results to the public. Such a view ignores the fact that colleges have always depended on the support of society, and that in return the community has asked institutional leaders (including the board of trustees) to account carefully for their use of resources.

Accountability does not rule out a degree of autonomy for the college. However, to fulfill the requirements of accountability, college officials need to explain how they are using this autonomy. Like the institutions they serve, college trustees are responsible to the public. This means that they should attend public functions and college events and take advantage of all appropriate activities to represent the board to the community. Leaders are responsible for communicating with the led.

### Legal, Educational, and Ethical Considerations

The values of legality, equity, honesty and openness, integrity, fidelity, loyalty, courtesy and respect, caring, excellence, and accountability make ethical decisions possible. However, effective decision making also requires ethical sensitivity and a method by which decisions can be reached. The identification and clarification of moral issues may be the most challenging aspect of ethical decision making. What situations or circumstances present the trustee with the need to make ethical decisions? In order to detect ethical issues in the matters their boards discuss, trustees must ask appropriate questions.

Effective discussions by boards have at least three dimensions: the legal, the educational, and the ethical. Because all three dimensions are essential, it is risky for a board to rely on one type of thinking to the exclusion of the others. For example, a trustee's chronic and unexcused absences at board meetings may be legal in most states, but they constitute irresponsible behavior and the board member will be judged accordingly.

Neither legal nor educational questions can consistently reveal ethical issues. For example, a trustee might discover that a group has an educational need that the college is in the best position to meet. If the trustee advocates meeting the need by bending the letter or spirit of the law or the canons of ethical behavior, he or she may set into motion a series of reckless, unethical actions. Such advocacy comes more easily than most trustees would like to admit. In 1991, a University of Illinois professor published a list of fifty-nine "illusory financial practices" that local governments use in Illinois to finance programs to serve the public (Picur, 1991). The fact that the funds are used for good purposes cannot offset the fact that they were raised through unethical practices. Similarly, an exercise of academic freedom that seriously injures a group of students violates the value of caring. These examples show that, unfortunately, ethical and educational considerations sometimes conflict.

To be responsible, trustees must continuously analyze issues from more than one perspective and attempt to select the course that best balances ethical, educational, and legal obligations. In this analysis, trustees should ask, Who is affected by the problem at hand? What is the board's responsibility to each of the parties? What possible solutions exist and what is the right thing to do? These questions should be posed early in the deliberations.

Unfortunately, ethical questions seldom produce universally acclaimed solutions. Just as educational, legal, and ethical considerations sometimes collide, so do ethical frameworks. In making ethical decisions, trustees occasionally face conflicts between equally cherished values. For example, a board chairperson may be torn between his or her duty to protect the privacy of a terminated employee (caring) and the duty to conduct the business of the college in a public fashion (openness). In most situations, all the values of the responsible life cannot be applied with equal weight. Nor do ethical judgments lend themselves to a simple calculus by which solutions are evaluated according to how many of the values are served.

### The Importance of Character and Reputation

The difficulty of ethical decision making often leaves trustees uncertain that they have made the right decision. Tough choices are open to debate, and not everyone will agree with the decisions of the board. In the long run, however, trustees with ethical sensitivity and competence establish a reputation for responsible behavior. Adherence to the value of integrity strengthens the governing board's confidence in itself and helps observers of the college and its board develop increased confidence in the character or moral profile of the board. The college community and the public are more likely to trust the decisions of trustees who have developed a reputation for responsible behavior.

Ethical leadership makes institutions strong. The reverse is true as well. Leadership is difficult for those who are suspected of moral deficiency. Therefore the wise trustee avoids even the appearance of unethical behavior. For example, when an unpaid trustee is offered an honorarium for making a speech at a local service club, he or she ought to think not only Is it right to accept? but also What is customary in these matters? and If I accept, will people who have placed their trust in me understand that it is right to do so?

### Disagreements on Ethical Issues Within the Board

Although most trustees and boards strive to operate ethically and to be above reproach, occasionally the president or members of a governing board find reason to question the behavior of a colleague. How should they proceed? The first step is to understand the basis of the colleague's behavior. Perhaps he or she is acting in conformity with a different value system than that of the other board members. If so, the board should discuss the issue and the value systems at work. On the other hand, the trustee may be the victim of a momentary lapse in judgment. Or the trustee may be unfamiliar with the values of the responsible life or ignorant of the demands of trusteeship.

Sometimes unethical behavior results from pressures that cause the trustee to retrogress in his or her judgment and actions. A trustee who feels insecure may want to establish his or her own importance by rejecting the authority embodied by a board chair or a majority of the board. At other times, peer pressure may overcome the trustee's better judgment and cause the trustee to act in ways that are ethically indefensible. The pressures of competition and the thrill of risk taking or winning also may contribute to unethical behavior.

Trustees may fail to exercise sound ethical judgment because they are unfamiliar with the values of the responsible life. If that is the case, the board chairperson (or if the chair is the problem, a senior member of the board) should counsel the colleague and explain the importance of board cohesiveness and responsible trusteeship. The board or the president may wish to call upon a trustees' association or another external consultant for assistance. The board member can be exposed to responsible values and behaviors through attending orientation sessions and trustee seminars and reading materials designed for governing boards.

Presidents must be careful not to assume too much of the responsibility for morally instructing trustees, who, as employers, sometimes resent the advice and retaliate. The responsibility for moral instruction belongs primarily to the chairperson and the other board members.

To resolve ethical conflict within a board, the chairperson should attempt to identify the cause of the controversial behavior that some members deem to be unethical. If the conflict is not severe, the concerned trustees might be justified in agreeing to tolerate the behavior. After all, reasonable people will occasionally disagree about ethical issues and can do so constructively. If the board is not comfortable accepting the questionable behavior of a colleague, it should try other approaches. It can use arguments to persuade the colleague to abandon his or her present course and adopt the position of the board. The board also can collaborate with the colleague in an attempt to find a mutually acceptable compromise.

Responsible board members find ways to put aside their personal differences for the good of the group. Should attempts at collaboration fail to provide an acceptable compromise for all those involved in the conflict, the board ought to negotiate or bargain. In negotiations, parties assume an adversarial relationship and bargain to reach agreement. Negotiations involve creativity as well as tension and can produce compromises that have eluded less formal efforts at collaboration.

Whenever a board confronts one of its own members over a purportedly unethical action, it is possible that the majority of the board members will change their position and endorse the values and behavior of the colleague. Such mass conversions are rare, but they do occur. However, the conflict is more likely to continue. In such cases, the board can attempt to compel the colleague in question to abandon his or her position and to identify and align with the board majority.

Board members could also try to initiate the recall of an

unethical colleague. In states like Illinois, however, no legal recourse exists for seeking the removal of unethical trustees. Thus the remaining members of a board must either resign themselves to living with disagreement or campaign (overtly or covertly) to remove the offender from office at the time of his or her bid for reelection or reappointment.

Offering political support for someone challenging an incumbent is risky. The incumbent could be returned to office despite the challenge and may seek revenge. Yet this type of action is not without precedent. Members of Congress, for example, often campaign against colleagues with whom they will have to work should their efforts fall short.

An attempt by the board to achieve unity on ethical matters is not a violation of the rights of others to believe as they see fit. The board is not depriving members in question of the opportunity to draw moral distinctions. Instead, it is asking that the member adjust his or her behaviors to make responsible board action possible.

Harmonious boards work to maintain a lively appreciation for their shared values. As new members are selected, the board chairperson and president should meet with them to discuss college affairs, including the values and beliefs of the previous board. The values and goals of the board also should be reviewed and evaluated at retreats and self-evaluation sessions. Finding ways to build, communicate, and preserve a relationship of mutual trust and shared values is a continuous and time-consuming process. With a commitment to a set of shared values, boards can consider problems from ethical as well as educational, financial, and legal perspectives.

When confronted by an especially difficult choice, a responsible board should feel free to seek the advice of a third party, a consultant, or a board mentor. The responsible board should neither rush to judgment in difficult situations nor delay acting until the action is irrelevant. Ethical boards realize that in most situations, the failure to act is itself an action.

The board's reputation is shaped by the way the trustees interact with college officers, employees, patrons, and students. Ethically mature boards have shared values, sensitivity to ethical issues, and a commitment to moral decision making. These boards develop a reputation for clear delegation, careful preparation, attentive consultation and communication, sound policy making, and regular self-evaluation. A high level of trust among its members and between the board and the chief executive officer typifies a successful board. Its members listen carefully to others' comments and recommendations. Outside advice is promptly summarized by the board chairperson or college president and considered by the board.

### Policies to Guide Ethical Decision Making

In weighing advice and reaching decisions, board members need to remember that clear policies can ensure fair and equitable treatment. According to traditional wisdom, boards make policy, and presidents administer the college accordingly. How can boards go about adopting policies that pass ethical muster?

Responsible boards challenge the president of their college to recommend policies that are consistent with the values of legality, equity, honesty and openness, integrity, fidelity, loyalty, courtesy and respect, caring, excellence, and accountability. Ethical boards also provide their presidents with the support they need to carry out the charges given. They do not expect the impossible, and they are quick to praise the president and the college when assignments are completed in a timely and satisfactory manner. They encourage the president and the other college leaders at appropriate times.

On the other hand, responsible boards do not hesitate to hold both the president and themselves accountable when goals are not achieved. They conduct regular evaluations, but in order to protect the trusting relationship between the board and the president, individual trustees do not conduct private investigations of presidential actions and behaviors. Board members report their concerns about matters that are the president's responsibility to the president promptly and privately. The president, in turn, reports to the board the outcome of his or her resulting inquiry into the matter in question. Through an agreed-upon division of labor, regular self-evaluation, and mutual support, a governing board and its president can demonstrate commitment to responsible, ethically informed governance.

College presidents live a paradox. They are simultaneously employees and teachers of the board. In their advisory capacity, presidents command an advantage in their relationship with trustees. In their evaluation and compensation of the president, boards have the advantage. If they do not handle this advantage carefully, boards can intimidate presidents and discourage courageous and creative recommendations. Tentative presidents lead to inactive, drifting boards and unresponsive colleges. To avoid this pitfall, responsible boards need to examine ways to strengthen the presidency through such devices as multiyear contracts, regular evaluation of the performance of the board and the president, and regular support for trustee and presidential development. Only by clarifying their expectations for the president can trustees encourage the kind of institutional leadership the college needs to thrive.

## Some Difficult Ethical Decisions for Boards

Not only do boards have the opportunity to select and charge new presidents, they also can influence their own makeup. By their college bylaws, many private college boards are self-perpetuating; they determine their own membership. Board members at public community colleges are usually elected or appointed by a government official. Even public boards, however, can influence their own membership by suggesting names to those making appointments or by encouraging certain people, overtly or covertly, to run for election to the board.

Is such involvement wise and ethical? The most convenient course in such matters is to abstain from involvement. Although inaction may be convenient, it may also represent a lost opportunity to improve the caliber of the board. In the past, public college trustees seldom became involved in the selection or election of their colleagues, but such involvement seems to be growing as more trustees take an active role in influencing the future makeup of their boards.

However, some types of involvement create conflicts of interest and therefore lack redeeming value. Trustees should not support candidates out of purely partisan loyalties. To do so would be to make the college an instrument of partisan politics, a means to an end rather than an end in itself. Nor should trustees seek personal gain through involvement in another's campaign. Although sitting trustees would be well equipped to market themselves as campaign managers in a community college election, to do so would damage their integrity by creating a conflict of interest. A trustee should not agree privately to support a colleague with the understanding that the favor will be returned and that certain offices of the board will be assigned as a reward for the support. Such agreements violate the value of openness and create an aura of suspicion within the board that makes trusting relationships and board cohesiveness nearly impossible to achieve.

Although making private deals for the office of board chairperson is unwise and unethical, trustees should become actively involved in the selection process of a chair because the chairperson plays a special role in guiding and directing the president and the board. Through the selection of a leader, the board can demonstrate a commitment to excellence.

To avoid conflict, some boards rotate the office of chairperson from member to member, based on seniority. Such a method has the advantage of exposing each trustee to the special responsibilities and vicissitudes of the office of chairperson. The rotation method may work for colleges whose trustees are equally suited by temperament, aspiration, and training to serve as the board chair. In reality, however, few colleges meet such a description.

To serve as an effective first-among-equals, a board chairperson should have the time and talent to monitor institutional issues closely, to consult frequently with the president, to ensure orientation for each trustee, and to ensure adequate communication with each board member. The effective board chair must be willing to confront and counsel a fellow board member immediately whenever that trustee's behavior causes political, legal, or ethical concern. The chairperson should be willing to lead the board through a regular process of self-examination with the specific purpose of improving the level of performance of the board. During board self-evaluation, chairs should solicit suggestions for improving board organization and their own performance.

Another area calling for wise board policy is planning and budgeting. Responsible boards expect presidents and their staff members to present program and fiscal recommendations, but they reserve for themselves the final task of balancing costs and benefits.

Trustees who wish to spend without regard for the limits on resources do not behave ethically. Conversely, it is irresponsible for trustees to seek to decrease college revenues while routinely ignoring expressions of institutional need. In financial discussions, ethically mature board members remind themselves of their responsibility to obey the law, treat taxpayers, students, and staff members fairly and consistently, hear and carefully consider the views of all affected parties, protect the public trust, and be accountable for the expenditure of all funds. For a responsible board, budget decisions not only are sound financially but also are sound politically and ethically.

Occasionally, boards must defend the autonomy of a college against those who would subvert it. Certain groups and political movements sometimes attempt to put colleges to work for a partisan cause. During the Second World War, the National Socialist (Nazi) party forced its beliefs on German schools and universities and removed nonconforming teachers from their posts. In the 1950s, teachers in the United States were sometimes fired for failing to take political oaths. Donors have attempted to use gifts to influence academic hiring and the programming at an institution. Such forms of coercion have threatened the academic freedom of teachers and students, and they have weakened colleges. Academic freedom is a treasure that distinguishes U.S. colleges and universities from those in some other countries. It can be successfully preserved only through the commitment of responsible governing boards.

The ethical board sees that the college honors its other commitments as well. Some of the principles a board is obligated to uphold are legally binding, but others are not. For example, a college may contract with a high school for classroom space needed to deliver instruction to students living at a great distance from the main campus. Once the contract expires, the college is legally free to end service to the site. In fact, declining enrollment trends might make discontinuation advisable.

One of the greatest challenges to boards is the need to change the college to adapt to emerging trends and needs. New directions and decisions by a board can conflict with the expectations created by past policy. Sooner or later, most trustees face situations in which commitments of previous boards collide with new and changing needs. In such situations, the boards should find out who would be affected by a change in college policy or plans. They should attempt to find a solution that moves the college forward while giving due consideration to all those who have come to rely on the directions adopted by previous boards.

## The Ethics of Reconsidering a Decision

After having done everything in their power to act responsibly, trustees occasionally have regrets about some of their decisions. What appeared right for the trustee or the board the week before may seem irresponsible in retrospect. What can the board members do when they have second thoughts about decisions? Some actions can be easily reconsidered and undone. Others cannot be reversed without undercutting public confidence in the board. Once a decision has been implemented, a reversal of the decision may bring harm to the college and the community.

When confronted by the ethical imperative to reconsider a decision, trustees should move cautiously and be careful not to make others pay for the exoneration of the board. If an apology by the board or a trustee is in order, the apology should be made. Even the reconsideration of a decision can become an opportunity for renewed commitment to governing responsibly and well.

From time to time, trustees may wish to reflect on their ethical obligations and performance. The reflection might begin with consideration of a trustee's code; several are readily available. While no code is perfect and trustees might enjoy writing their own, the code at the end of the chapter summarizes much of the discussion in this chapter.

## Reference

Picur, R. D. *Local Government Fiscal Practices in Illinois: From Stewardship and Accountability to Smoke and Mirrors.* Springfield: Taxpayers' Federation of Illinois, 1991.

## Exhibit 1. The Trustee's Code.

*I promise to fulfill my role by*

1. Studying my legal responsibilities
2. Advising, counseling, and supporting but not undercutting or second-guessing the president
3. Informing the president immediately of any concerns regarding performance, conduct, or style that, in the opinion of the board, require the president's attention
4. Participating fully in evaluations of the performance of both the president and the board
5. Supporting and counseling the board chairperson
6. Supporting the quest for excellence
7. Defining and regularly reexamining the college mission
8. Insisting on adequate orientation for new members of the board
9. Striving to put the good of society and the college district above all else

*I promise to decide policy on the basis of
law, logic, and reliable information by*

1. Insisting that the president keep all board members fully informed about vital issues facing the college and the board
2. Asking the president to present the board with documented recommendations on all issues requiring board decisions
3. Studying board materials submitted to the board by the president
4. Asking for presidential analysis of critical comments by faculty members, students, and others and suggesting that critics use channels before coming to the board
5. Insisting that the president provide opportunities for the board to hear from various college and community constituencies

*I pledge loyalty to the board by*

1. Respecting each board colleague
2. Protecting confidential material
3. Supporting all board decisions, even those I did not favor initially
4. Insisting that the chairperson alone speak for the board when it is not in session
5. Fostering trustee development activities with my presence and budgetary support
6. Listening to the needs of all constituencies and refusing to function as the agent for special interests or for partisan political groups
7. Avoiding personal statements that might be construed as commitments on behalf of the board
8. Contributing to a board environment in which controversial issues are presented fairly and in which the dignity of each individual is recognized and protected
9. Avoiding public utterances or actions that would discredit the board and undermine public confidence in the college or damage its reputation

## Exhibit 1. The Trustee's Code, cont'd.

10. Providing the board and the president with appropriate advance notice of my absences or my plans to resign or seek another position
11. Resigning whenever I am unable to fulfill my duties for more than a twelve-week period

*I promise to avoid all conflicts of interest by*

1. Apprising the board of any possible conflict of interest at the earliest opportunity
2. Refraining from voting on any issue in which I have a financial interest or on any issue on which I have given my professional advice to the college or board
3. Suggesting that the board use a third party rather than seeking my professional opinion on matters falling within my area of expertise
4. Refusing to use my position on the board for the financial gain of my family, business partners, personal friends, or myself
5. Refusing to represent any single constituency on the board
6. Refusing to request that the college hire any individual

**Part Three**

# Ensuring the Highest Standards of Leadership

# Chapter Eight

# Selecting and Developing
# Community College Leaders

## Charles B. Neff

One of the most important tasks of any community college is to select and evaluate its leaders. At the apex of that general task is the choice of a college president. Inevitably, many interests and individuals will influence that choice. How can they best play their roles in an ethical manner?

I write this chapter from the perspective of a thirty-year career in higher education and with recent involvement in more than twenty-five presidential searches. These searches have included a variety of institutions, including community colleges.

Let me now begin with an operational definition of the term *ethical practice* that will serve throughout this chapter as the basis for measuring whether particular actions in the choice and evaluation of a president are ethical. This definition and the use of it in the discussion that follows are in general agreement with the advice and analysis offered by Nason (1984b) and by McLaughlin and Riesman (1990).

### A Definition of Ethical Practice

All educational institutions, public or private, serve a public pur- pose stated in the mission of the institution. A major expression

171

of the ethos and ethics of an institution is the method by which the institution chooses a chief executive and the degree to which that chief executive is personally and professionally capable of leading the institution in the fulfillment of its public mission. Ethical practice, in this context, means that the stated purposes of the presidential search and the conducting of the search are consistent internally and also consistent with the mission of the institution.

A presidential search process is ethical if

- The design of the search process is consistent with the public mission of the institution.
- The implementation of the search process is consistent with the public mission of the institution.
- All groups affected by the outcome of the process have some influence on the search process.

The evaluation of the president's performance is ethical if the performance is assessed in terms of its consistency with the mission of the institution and with the specific criteria used in the selection of the president.

These standards assume that the most important ethical task performed by a community college is providing high-quality education to its students in fulfillment of the public trust of those constituencies that support the college in its mission. A search for a president should thus be a reflection of the mission of an institution. In a presidential search, the mission is translated into practice, not just reflected in rhetoric. The statements and practices of an institution during the selection of a president carry over into the evaluation of that president's performance. It is the congruence of all these elements—a clear statement of the mission, a search process consistent with the mission, and an evaluation of performance consistent with the criteria utilized in that search—that can be judged as ethical practice.

Ethical practice is best achieved through a well-planned and public selection process. After all, community colleges are public institutions. Their leadership is charged with a public trust and must demonstrate that trust through its actions. This trust is linked to fulfillment of the educational mission of the institution. It follows, therefore, that the expectations of the various publics served by a particular community college must to some degree be honored not only by the choice of a leader but also in the means by which the leader is chosen.

Local politics certainly has a place in the choice of a president. The president must be able to relate to groups and individuals who will make the crucial decision about financial support. The personal preferences of board members also play a part in the selection process. Board members must, after all, work closely with the president and be able to trust his or her judgment. But there are limits on the roles that politics and personal preference can and should play.

A board that pays attention only to politics may choose a president adept in the political arena but at odds with the faculty members. The quality of education suffers. A board that chooses only someone with whom it feels comfortable will probably choose someone similar to the board members. Opportunity and diversity suffer. A board that does not consult all constituent groups and find means for negotiating agreement among conflicting groups through the process of selecting a president will probably pass on the conflicts, sometimes in worse form, to the new president. The new president will be mired in conflict instead of being able to address change and growth.

I do not think it is possible or desirable to develop a single test to identify leaders who are ethical or distinguish them from those who are not. Nor could we develop a single list of practices that are ethical per se. In this country, we are uncomfortable with prescription and with ideological tests of correctness, whether conservative or liberal. Our best institutions and our most effective leaders emerge from a process of consensus building and accommodation.

Do these views avoid the issue of an individual's ethical record and performance? No, and they do not have that intention. They do suggest, however, that an individual can be best judged, and perhaps only judged, if institutional processes are ethical. A search process that results from agreement among constituents about the purpose of the search and balances that purpose in subsequent actions will be the process most likely to identify the most ethical individuals.

This chapter does not address in detail the means by which personal reference checks are carried out on presidential candidates. Some very reliable techniques exist to make such inquiries. But all of these techniques depend on clear institutional self-awareness and a consistent search process. It is relatively easy to determine whether an individual is ethical if the basis for that determination is adequately reflected in the institution and its practices.

In the remainder of this chapter, I will examine the practices most likely to produce ethical or unethical results in the choice and evaluation of a president. In particular, I will examine the following: establishing the process for presidential search, meeting the requirements of affirmative action, considering internal candidates, and assessing presidential performance. These particular issues do not constitute all of the circumstances in which an institution faces ethical questions during a search for a president. But they are the ones that often create the most problematic ethical conflicts. Careful attention to them through a well-considered process will reduce the possibility of ethical difficulties in other areas as well, including final judgments about the ethics of individual candidates.

## Ethical Practice in Establishing the Search Process

In setting up a process to identify and appoint a new president of a community college, a board and those individuals working with it will be well advised to review the three basic elements of the search process: selection, screening, and searching (or identification of candidates). The board should consider first what is actually the last part of the process, the selection of the president. Selection is a board responsibility, and in exercising that responsibility, the board can stumble ethically in two important ways.

First, the board members can stumble by moving directly to selection without giving adequate attention to searching and screening. As a result, the candidate pool may be extremely limited by the immediate preference of the board, perhaps even limited to one individual. The board then has no opportunity to consider alternative candidates or, even more important, to discuss the reasons that other individuals should be considered.

The second way in which the board can err ethically is to give away its responsibility. The charter and the bylaws that establish a board charge its members with explicit responsibilities and grant them, collectively, certain powers. Selection of a president is always one of these responsibilities. The board must not give away that responsibility or its powers but rather must exercise them ethically.

Powerful outside groups and individuals or inside groups and individuals, often equally powerful, will wish to usurp the responsibility of the board in making the final selection of a president. But if a board is to function as the guardian of the public trust, it must not diminish its own powers. It must exercise its responsibility for choosing the president rather than cede it to others.

In exercising its responsibility to choose the president, a board may properly and ethically delegate parts of the search process to other groups or individuals. A board may, for example, establish a group independent of but responsible to the board to supervise both the screening of and the search for candidates. These two functions are usually combined in a search and screening committee (hereafter called a search committee) on which the board as well as other constituencies are represented. The board must, at a minimum, establish a mechanism for searching for candidates and preferably a mechanism for screening candidates as well. These processes should involve individuals beyond the membership of the board.

Why is it ethical for the board to establish such mechanisms? First, a board, however representative, can in practice begin to operate like a closed club. In a presidential search, the clubhouse doors must be opened so that someone other than a club member, or someone other than a person known only to club members, has the chance of being the next president. Legal requirements for equal opportunity alone require that, except in unusual circumstances, all individuals who wish to be considered for a presidency be given open and fair consideration. Second, since the board represents a public trust, its members should be cognizant of and consider the desires of the public it serves. A board always has the option of evaluating, accepting, or rejecting suggestions, but it first has an obligation to consider them.

In choosing a president, a board is not just naming an individual. It is, through the qualities represented by that individual, saying something about the nature of the institution and what the institution can and should be. Virtually every group within the college's purview—its current and future students, its alumni, the people in the immediate community served by the college—will be affected by the president's actions. Since so many groups and individuals will be affected, it seems not merely expedient but also ethically proper to allow them a voice in the selection process, that is, to consider their viewpoints in determining the qualities sought in the next president and to invite them to share in the process of seeking candidates.

Different groups can be brought into the search process in a number of different ways. Broad representation by different groups (faculty members, students, alumni) on a search committee is the most common way, although use of a board committee as the search committee, assisted by an additional advisory committee, is not uncommon.

Regardless of the committee structure, one group in particular cannot be ignored—the faculty members. Neglect of the faculty members in the search process can work to the disadvantage of a new president, who may not be accepted by or function well with the faculty. The faculty is not an ordinary group of employees. Unfortunately, some legislators or board members make the mistake of thinking in such terms, especially when a union contract governs faculty-institution relations. The quality of the education that the college provides ultimately depends upon the preparation, ability, and enthusiasm of faculty members. A presidential search process that ignores or demeans faculty members may alienate them from the new president and make them less effective in their primary task.

By contrast, if faculty members participate effectively in a search, an atmosphere of acceptance and trust can be engendered even before a new president arrives. A good search process finds a constructive role for the faculty members in the best interests of the institution as a whole.

## Ethical Practice in Implementing the Search Process

The board must establish or instruct a group to establish on its behalf clear criteria for the qualities sought in a new president. The search process should relate exclusively to those qualities identified and not to others that a search committee, a board, or indeed any other members of the campus community may wish to include at some later point. It is crucial that the criteria be explicitly established early in the process.

*Screening* is the process of applying the criteria established by the board or by the search committee on behalf of the board. Screening is normally delegated to a search committee. In screening, the established leadership criteria are used to reduce a large number of applicants to a smaller number of semifinalists and ultimately to a group of finalists.

At each stage of the search process, the search committee must make sure that it is applying the original criteria and that no major additional ones have been added. For example, the statement of leadership criteria will often contain a reference to educational requirements. These requirements are often open so as not to be too restrictive. They may state that the president should have educational attainment consistent with that of the faculty. But restrictions may either be assumed or introduced as the process goes forward. If a doctoral degree has not been established as a basis for selection, it should not be later introduced as a requirement. Sometimes, for example, the committee will determine that the president should be a doctor of philosophy rather than a doctor of education even though the criteria state only that the president have an earned doctorate.

Occasionally, personal criteria will creep into the process as it develops. For example, has it been assumed all along that the candidate will be married and have a spouse who (though unpaid) will be deeply involved in the life of the college? Is it implicitly expected that the candidate will be male or will have the correct political affiliations?

There are also more subtle forms of unstated criteria. Is it assumed, for instance, that the president must be acceptable to the culture of a particular geographic region? Within some limits and all other things being equal, it is wise for the board to assure that a candidate can operate within a particular political or regional culture. But if these considerations are preeminently important, they should be explicitly stated by the board and the search committee early in the process. If the committee believes an individual should, for example, be familiar by experience with rural Tennessee, that criterion should be made explicit in materials sent to candidates.

Prospective candidates must know the real rules of a search process, and those rules must be applied fairly and consistently. After all, people are often taking quite a chance in applying. They are investing a considerable amount of their time and energy, especially if they become semifinalists or finalists. It is unfair to them and a form of unethical practice by the institution if unstated or hidden selection criteria are allowed to become the real basis for the final selection of a president.

### Confidentiality

Confidentiality is another area that a board must consider in the selection process. A great deal of attention has been given to this area in recent years, and strong partisan views have emerged. Scholars disagree about how much openness is desirable, whether disclosure should occur early in the process, or whether it is only when finalists are named that their identities should be revealed (McLaughlin and Riesman, 1989; Cleveland, 1985). Different states have differing rules about openness. For public institutions, no board or search committee can operate outside the requirements of the law, although current cases in the courts are still defining the actual requirements and limits of openness in many local situations. Requirements about open meetings and access to information are often beyond the control of a board.

One aspect of confidentiality, however, is within the control of an institution—the relationship of the institution to the candidates. It would seem both fair and ethical to keep the candidates informed throughout all stages in the process about the degree of confidentiality they can expect. If an institution can promise a certain degree of confidentiality to candidates, it should make that guarantee early in the process. If it cannot promise confidentiality, that message should also be clear. Candidates then know how much they must risk by entering the search process.

A board or its committee may find in the course of a search

that it has to reveal information about the candidates that it did not wish to reveal. Candidates trust that institutions will abide by their promises. If candidates are later surprised by public disclosure of their names, they are sometimes hurt professionally and often are angry. Pressure by the press or a new interpretation of regulations may require that a board or committee reveal information about candidates during the search process. If the rules of confidentiality change, it certainly is not ethical for a board or a search committee to withhold that information from candidates in an effort to keep candidates in a pool.

### Community Involvement

If the rules of selection and a clear statement of criteria for screening are in place, the search for candidates can be conducted with total openness. If selecting candidates is the function of the board and screening is the function of the search committee, then searching for candidates ought to involve the entire academic community. An active, widespread search can only occur if everyone knows the kind of individual whom the board and the search committee are seeking and if all people in the community are given as much information about the search process as is possible, consistent with maintaining confidentiality.

One excellent device to involve the academic community in searching for candidates is to publish and widely circulate the statement of leadership criteria. The institution thus demonstrates that it is willing to make its screening and selection criteria public and, by implication, is willing to be held accountable for the application of those criteria in the ensuing process. The selection of one person among several finalists is, inevitably, based on judgment. The campus community is less likely to deny the board its prerogative to make that judgment and more likely to give it the latitude to arrive at the judgment if the selection criteria have been published and a process has been established that appears certain to apply those criteria in an equitable manner.

### Ethical Practice and Affirmative Action

An institution must carry out the requirements of affirmative action; it must comply with what is mandated by law. But educational opportunity truly cannot be increased through a simple response to legal requirements alone. Affirmative action is the floor upon which a policy based on equity can be built. That policy, in turn, is one that responds to the need for what might better be called *affirmative opportunity*.

Perhaps no other area presents more possibilities for ethical dilemmas than affirmative action. Over time, this term has ceased to be very precise because it invites so many different interpretations. For some individuals, affirmative action is a social responsibility. For others, it is a legal burden. Some people see affirmative action as an ethical quagmire that may bog down an institution in actions and reactions and produce difficult and costly court cases. In fact, affirmative action as it is practiced and enforced is all of these things: a responsibility, a requirement, and a potential danger. It is also an important opportunity, though that aspect of affirmative action is all too often obscured.

In sorting out the ethical dimensions of affirmative action, a clear distinction should be made between what is required and what can and, indeed, ethically should be done. I use the term *affirmative action* to mean a requirement for redress of inequity, a connotation it by and large already possesses. To address the issue of what can and should be done, I will use the term *affirmative opportunity*.

Affirmative action is basically a set of antidiscrimination provisions. An institution cannot, except under special circumstances, carry out a closed search for job candidates. It must announce a position openly, and it may not legally discriminate against applicants on the basis of race, gender, religion, age, or national origin. Furthermore, the processes of screening and selection must not operate to eliminate certain categories of individuals, formally or informally. A number of personal questions relating to gender, religion, race, marital status, and age are explicitly proscribed.

Usually, a community college, in response to affirmative action requirements, advertises a position in the *Chronicle of Higher Education* as well as in other sources. The institution announces that it is an Equal Employment Opportunity and Affirmative Action (EEO/AA) employer and establishes a search committee with at least some female and minority members. It then waits for a diverse pool of applicants to respond, only to be amazed that very few minorities and women enter its applicant pool. Even when the pool includes minorities and women, after initial screening (particularly if a numerical rating is used that gives so many points for each category and is totaled for each individual), no women or minorities may emerge as finalists.

The institution might include the provision in its search criteria that a minority group member or a woman must be included in the group of finalists. But this requirement might be made without any additional effort to change the applicant pool. As a result, unqualified individuals may become finalists, only, predictably, to be eliminated when a final decision occurs. Or perhaps the institution, faced with an all-white or all-male group of finalists, instructs a search committee to enrich the pool, usually after other semifinalists have been chosen. Selected individuals are "discovered," although at that stage in the process it is difficult to locate individuals who match the leadership criteria. Those people added to the group are later eliminated.

In all such cases the results are the same; it is difficult for minorities and women to become viable candidates. The flaw in these methods is that the institution is operating only on the basis of the requirements of affirmative action, not ethics. Thus neither affirmative opportunity nor the issue of real intent receives attention early in the process, and virtually no gains are made by the underrepresented groups. The attempts to find candidates were merely reactions to requirements rather than active efforts to promote ethical policy and the social good.

Candidates who are put through such a process repeatedly become cynical. They come to believe that they have been included only as window dressing and that the institution never seriously intended to consider them as candidates. Within the institution, a kind of backlash often occurs. Affirmative action appears to be merely a bureaucratic requirement. It seems to be a nuisance that is not related (in fact, is often opposed) to quality, something to be responded to minimally, quickly, and if possible painlessly.

To engage in a policy of affirmative opportunity requires a board, its search committee, and indeed a whole academic community to take a very different approach toward the issues generally lumped under the term *affirmative action* (American Council on

Education, 1986). Openly advertising positions or refraining from asking certain questions are good practices, but they are not the same as creating real opportunities for underrepresented groups. A campus must not only be willing to accept different kinds of candidates (those who, in whatever terms, are deemed nontraditional) but must also be eager to enjoy the benefits of diversity. Often, to create a climate in which diversity is valued will require campuswide education about the positive advantages of adding to the institution perspectives and experiences not now represented. Recognition of the benefits of diversity for the campus as well as the candidates will help to create such an environment.

A board and a search committee should spend time discussing in public what they mean by affirmative action (or affirmative opportunity) before a search gets under way. Such discussions will either produce or fail to produce a sense of conviction that nontraditional candidates are welcome for the post of president. If this conviction does not exist at the outset, no process is subsequently likely to kindle it in the course of a presidential search.

Demonstrating such a conviction requires more than going through conventional motions. Understandably, some of the best nontraditional candidates will not enter a search without assurance that they have a genuine chance of getting the position and that they are not being invited to participate as tokens. These candidates are unlikely to respond to advertising alone. There is no substitute for active contacts with people who are aware of available candidates and, beyond that, direct discussion with the candidates themselves.

Most candidates, including minority candidates, want to know the actual situation at an institution. They are not impressed by high-flown rhetoric or philosophical statements of educational opportunity unaccompanied by positive action. Strong candidates want to know that a real opportunity exists for them and that the institution is honest and serious about its willingness to accomplish what it says it wants to do. They also want to know that the search and selection processes will be ethical.

## Ethical Practice and Internal Candidates

How to handle internal candidates in a presidential search is another ethical issue. By following some basic principles, a board is likely to act ethically in this matter.

If there is an obvious strong internal candidate, one whom the board unanimously wants as the next president, the board should name that individual immediately. To be sure, following this course can be dangerous. If there is any doubt whatsoever that the board is considering naming anyone other than the best and strongest candidate, the board should not select its internal candidate. If, however, the board is confident in its convictions, it is more advisable for the board to move expeditiously, explain its actions thoroughly, and take whatever repercussions may be forthcoming than to go through a process whose results are a foregone conclusion. Furthermore, if there is a foregone conclusion and any process is later initiated that implies otherwise, the credibility of the board and the internal candidate is compromised.

This advice may seem to contradict the previous argument for a thorough and open search. An internal candidate should be appointed without a search only under unusual circumstances. If a president departs unexpectedly or dies, leaving significant and ongoing commitments that require continuous direction, and if establishing an acting or interim presidency would appear to create a damaging hiatus, the board may find it prudent to immediately appoint a strong and qualified insider as the next president. The board should be very sure, however, that the person it chooses will provide better long-term as well as short-term leadership than anyone else available.

Barring the immediate choice of an insider under unusual circumstances, it is best to include insiders in an open search like other candidates. Treating internal candidates differently from other candidates involves both the board and the candidates in potentially difficult ethical situations. Board members may have an understandable desire to acknowledge the success of administrators and faculty leaders and an equally commendable desire not to hurt their feelings. As laudable as those instincts are, they create ethical dilemmas for all concerned if the board members act upon them in the search for a president.

An institution should thus avoid any guarantee to a certain class of administrators (vice president or above, for example) or, worse yet, to all internal candidates, that they will be interviewed as semifinalists. Such a guarantee has unfortunate effects. It signals to people on the outside that the job may be reserved for an internal candidate. Even when that is not the case, the resulting ambiguity about the status of internal versus external candidates may cause some excellent external prospects to hesitate to enter the process.

This type of guarantee often has a deleterious effect on the internal candidates themselves also. Some individuals will interpret the decision to guarantee interviews as indication of a favored position in the process. Despite all negative information, human beings tend to engage in wishful thinking. Consequently, a candidate who could have been let down gently early in the search builds up hopes and is even more disappointed when at the semifinalist stage the inevitable message is finally conveyed. At the very least, a search committee should inform interviewees that all will receive equal consideration and that all will be assessed in accordance with the published leadership criteria. One set of rules for certain candidates and a different set for others is neither good nor ethical practice.

By guaranteeing semifinalist status to internal candidates, the institution is also denying semifinalist positions to other candidates who may be more qualified. This practice can be particularly harmful to minority and female candidates, thus doubling the ethical damage. There simply is a numerical limit to the number of semifinalists a search committee can consider. There are only so many hours in a day, so many days that a search committee can be held together, and so many candidates who can be interviewed. To accommodate more people, interviews will of necessity be abbreviated and thus be less valuable, or else the search committee's attention span will be stretched and its concentration diminished. In either case, the committee does a less effective job of screening.

Internal candidates should expect and be accorded the same degree of confidentiality enjoyed by other candidates. On a campus, especially a small one, the candidacy of internal staff members may be hard to mask. Individuals will occasionally announce their own candidacy and campaign on campus. These campaigns are difficult for a search committee to handle, but a firm policy of treating all candidates equally is still the best response.

### Ethical Practice and Evaluations of Performance

The basis for the evaluation of a president's performance is actually put in place during a presidential search, for it is during the search process that expectations about presidential performance are first stated. All too often, those expectations are implicit or at least not explicit enough. As a result, the expectations may change subtly, even substantially, during a president's tenure. Or they may be too vague to serve as a useful basis for evaluation. Explicitness and a common understanding by all parties form the basis for an ethical evaluation of a president.

A well-conceived and executed search process will ensure that the board and the new president work together to promote the same purposes at the same institution. On the face of it, that statement may seem obvious or even trivial, but it is neither. In fact, the statement points to an issue that, if not addressed, can evolve into an ethical problem of considerable dimensions.

During a search for a president, the board must strive to describe accurately the condition of the institution it oversees and equally accurately its expectations for the performance of the president. Otherwise, consciously or unconsciously, the board may hire a president with expectations for one kind of institution while the board possesses very different expectations. Such a situation inevitably leads to conflict over goals and administrative practices. If the board appears to be saying that it wants one style of leadership and in fact expects a different style, the president will at best be confused and at worst will be evaluated on standards different from those originally stated. Either way, the situation leads to trouble and usually to deteriorating board-president relations and even to termination of the president's tenure.

No institution wants to search for a president any more often than necessary. Whatever can be done to reduce the possibility of the board and the president working at cross-purposes is to the advantage of the board and the institution, not to mention the president. The development of good working relations between the board and the president begins during the search process and is related to three important elements. The first is an open evaluation of the current condition of the institution, its major problems as well as its opportunities. The second is the transmission of that information in an unambiguous way to all candidates. The third is a clear statement to candidates of the board's expectations for future performance of the president.

To be clear about its current condition, including board-president relations, the institution should conduct a self-study in areas of particular difficulty, for instance, in admissions or records, financial practices, or academic quality. The search committee should decide early what type of information it will share with candidates. It may decide to send only public information—a catalogue, a student viewbook, a collection of recent newspaper articles about the college—to all applicants and nominees. For semifinalists, it may add a copy of the faculty handbook and at least the summary portion of the latest accreditation report as well as institutional research on student characteristics. For finalists, the financial records of the institution should be totally open, especially data on assets, capital projects, the management of the budget, and faculty personnel practices. In fact, the board should probably even highlight particular problems as a way of demonstrating its openness and its willingness to work with a new president in their resolution.

If the board and the search committee are willing to face problems honestly and to present honest information to candidates, the strongest candidates probably will emerge. Individuals who want a soft berth will be more likely to steer clear of an institution with real problems. On the other hand, some of the best candidates will be intrigued. They may welcome an opportunity to solve problems and to make a difference in the institution through their solutions.

After presenting an open and accurate picture of the college to potential candidates, the board can with equal honesty make a similar statement about expectations of the new president. Institutions commonly know, in general terms, what they wish to accomplish in the future, and these desires are usually expressed in a long-range plan. A well-conducted search will also give a board a fairly clear picture of the kind of leader it seeks. But often an important mediating element is missing: an explicit statement of expectations about those areas in which the board would like the leader to focus in the near future, including providing ethical leadership.

One way of correcting this deficiency is for the board to develop a statement of several paragraphs addressing the four or five areas on which it would most like the new president to concentrate during the first contractual period. Such a statement provides direction for the president. And through drafting it, the board achieves a greater degree of consensus on expectations than it might have had previously. In such a statement, the board and the president also possess a clear basis for evaluation. Unless expectations are explicitly spelled out before the president takes office, true evaluation of performance is difficult.

If the expectations have been well stated, the resulting evaluation process follows a by-now-obvious path. A great deal has been written about presidential assessment, giving the board several choices about mechanisms (Hays, 1976; Munitz, 1980; Nason, 1984a; Seldin, 1988). In general, a good evaluative process is founded on clear expectations, and its mechanisms should have three related parts.

First, the board chair should be in regular communication with the president, receiving and reacting to information without crossing the line that separates the setting of policy from the day-to-day administration of the institution. The chairperson should be willing to keep the president regularly informed about the board's understanding of the president's performance, just as the president should keep the chair informed about major developments at the college.

The president should hear from the board chair when the board is satisfied with a particularly good accomplishment. Similarly, the president should be informed whenever he or she deviates from expectations. This kind of informal communication will assist the president in making minor corrections before major ones are needed. Furthermore, the president will be able to operate in an atmosphere of confidence, knowing, in the absence of statements to the contrary, that his or her performance is satisfactory to the board. Performance then is perceived by both sides as adhering to the expectations upon which the board and the president have mutually agreed. Informal consultation is the first level of evaluation.

Second, the board should formally review the president's performance each year and perhaps link that review to salary increases. Often this review is conducted by the executive committee on behalf of the board.

Third, the board may wish to consider establishing a formal

review associated with contract renewal or its equivalent. That process should be agreed to by both the board and the incumbent president. It should be announced well in advance of an actual evaluation so that instituting it does not imply that the board has discovered something wrong that it wants to correct through evaluation. The use of an outsider in this review process is often helpful and strengthens the process.

## Conclusion

Community colleges are established to serve the public good in specific ways—improving people's minds, adding occupational skills to society, providing an educational avenue for equal opportunity. Through its support for those goals, the public is, in effect, ratifying them as desirable, ethical intentions. Those intentions are realized in large measure through the quality of the individuals chosen to lead these institutions. They are further realized when the leaders of community colleges are evaluated in light of public expectations.

A community college should be clear and open in all aspects of presidential selection and evaluation, sure and committed in its own intentions. It should select leaders who are suited to the college and its mission, opportunities, and problems. Ethical practice in presidential search requires consistency between what an institution says it is (its mission statement), what it wishes to be (its statement about leadership expectations), and the means by which it implements a search process. When these are in place, candidates can be screened to ensure that they have the highest ethical suitability as individuals. If a community college engages in these practices, it is providing the best guarantee that all of its leaders—its board, its faculty members, its administration—will function as an ethical whole.

## References

American Council on Education. *Deciding Who Shall Lead.* Washington, D.C.: American Council on Education, 1986.

Cleveland, H. *The Costs and Benefits of Openness: Sunshine Laws and Higher Education.* Washington, D.C.: Association of Governing Boards, 1985.

Hays, G. "'Evaluating a President: The Minnesota Plan." *AGB Reports,* 1976, *18*(5), 5–9.

McLaughlin, J. B., and Riesman, D. "The Shady Side of Sunshine: The Press and Presidential Searches." *Change,* 1989, *21*(1), 44–57.

McLaughlin, J. B., and Riesman, D. *Choosing a College President.* Princeton, N.J.: Carnegie Foundation for the Advancement of Teaching, 1990.

Munitz, B. "Reviewing Presidential Leadership." In R. T. Ingram and Associates, *Handbook of College and University Trusteeship: A Practical Guide for Trustees, Chief Executives, and Other Leaders Responsible for Developing Effective Governing Boards.* San Francisco: Jossey-Bass, 1980.

Nason, J. W. *Presidential Assessment.* Washington, D.C.: Association of Governing Boards, 1984a.

Nason, J. W. *Presidential Search.* Washington, D.C.: Association of Governing Boards, 1984b.

Seldin, P. "How to Evaluate Campus Executives." *AGB Reports,* 1988, *30*(5), 16–19.

━━━━━ **Chapter Nine** ━━━━━

# The Importance of Ethics in Good Administrative Practices

## James B. Tatum

The insights provided by the writers of earlier chapters in this book are particularly valuable. In addition to illuminating the ethical pitfalls that plague educational leadership, each writer challenges college leaders to move to a higher level of ethical practice. Ethical growth requires that college leaders see things as wholly as possible and reach an understanding that will result in a more ideal environment in which to prepare people to live in our increasingly complex world.

Stimulated by the words of Gus Tyler, assistant president and political director of the International Ladies' Garment Workers' Union, I have attempted in this chapter to respond to this challenge by my colleagues and to try to create a vision of ethical rightness. I do not claim exclusivity to this vision. It has wisely been said that there is nothing new in this world. Certainly, other people have made this conceptual journey before I undertook it. It is true, however, that when we have that "aha!" moment—when the thought becomes our own—the thought is entirely fresh.

Tyler (1991), in addressing the issues of our day, said, "How can we overcome our tendency to focus narrowly and learn to widen our vision to absorb the myriad influences on people and societies coming from all parts of the universe? The answer may lie in our ability to conceptualize—to condense detailed data into abstractions, inventing a word or a formula that transforms into a simple, understandable unit a plethora of items" (p. 35).

Tyler's words touched me at the deepest level, and I committed to attempt to deal with the issue of ethics using such a process. Because I value so highly the work of Michael Josephson of the Josephson Institute for the Advancement of Ethics I am repeating his list of principles and am suggesting that the reader review the discussion of the principles in Chapter Seven. Briefly, Josephson believes that people should be honest, have integrity, keep promises, possess fidelity, be fair, care about others, respect others, be responsible citizens, work for excellence, be accountable for their actions, and protect the public trust.

## Trust as an Icon

Contemplating the ethical values and principles advocated by Tyler and Josephson with a view toward choosing those that seem most meaningful brings about a deeper understanding of each of the values and how they are intertwined. It is possible to include some values as part and parcel of one another and to determine which value is supreme. The exercise of identifying the most important value causes the chooser to have an encompassing vision of what that choice means. It is possible that such thinking will lead to another word or phrase that has a broader, deeper meaning than those words used earlier to describe Josephson's values.

I have chosen the word *trust* to describe the supreme value because it connects us all in a common but important way. It is a word that describes the results of actions conforming to all of the listed values. It has both an experiential meaning and an intuitive one. *Intuition* in this case could be defined as a memory of the truth, carrying the ring of authenticity.

If trust is all that I believe that it is, it could well be viewed much as an icon is used in religious observance. The image the word conveys is representative of deeper, more complex understandings. Think of it this way. Suppose every decision is prefaced with deliberate questions—Will this build trust? Will it build long-term trust? How might it destroy trust? Such a simple approach is not so simple. It means that we have the obligation to train our mind to encompass all of the values with one vision and have an ability to apply the issue of building trust.

### Lessons from Previous Chapters

To increase trust and to develop the widest range of ethical responsibility, college leaders must truly understand some issues raised by the preceding writers. The previous chapters illuminate the importance of recognizing two categories of ethical failure. People who fail ethically either know better but do not do better or are not aware of wrongdoing. Undoubtedly, there are degrees of knowing or not knowing. Some people may be nagged by a vague uneasiness as they make a decision. Some could have no realization of wrongdoing. Some could make a decision and say in hindsight, "I knew better than that." And some people could deliberately make a decision knowing it was wrong.

In the wake of the savings and loan scandal in the United States in 1990, a national wire service quoted Senator Alan Cranston as saying, "If I had known what I know now, I wouldn't have done it." This statement expresses very well the acuity of hindsight. Such a statement by a public person who has achieved so much should cause us sober reflection. It is also a statement that many of us could have made and perhaps have made in our lifetime and it suggests that we must come to grips with this thing called ethics.

It is likely that more people either know better or at least have uneasy feelings about their actions than have no sense of wrongdoing. Therefore, an important theme that emerges from some of the writers in this book is one of choosing to do what one knows to be right. Most administrators, if asked hypothetically, "Would you employ an individual because he or she comes highly recommended by a financial donor?" would respond either by saying no or by saying, "I need some more information." Actually, in a real situation, some would find ways to justify hiring the person no matter what. The same denial can occur when presidents choose to institute certain questionable business and industrial training programs to increase funding from the state. In the isolation of a classroom discussion on this subject in graduate school, most if not all people would choose the high road. However, if a front-page newspaper article appeared about either of the above situations, we would read the same remark that Cranston made. It is evident that we often know better but do not do better.

It is important to acknowledge that we are not as sensitive as we might be. More specifically, our ability to see with fullness the ramifications of certain decisions is not as acute as it might be. For example, many of the leaders of women's groups readily admit that their own speaking and writing has not always been free of sexist language. Certainly, this is true of men. Our awareness of the use of sexist language has been heightened through education. The same is true of our understanding of racial issues. It seems, therefore, that ethical decision making can be vastly improved through educational processes. Still, all too many people know better but do not do better. It would seem that the answer to both knowing and doing lies in intense and frequent discussions and focus on ethics.

The previous chapters have also given us a renewed impetus to focus on certain key points. One of those is the need to understand the mission of the college fully and to develop a high sense of maintaining a mission with integrity. The entire campus community must understand the mission and the purpose underlying the mission. The writers in this book seem to say that the mission of the community college is to be committed to actualizing people to their fullest as human beings. Colleges truly are about the business of helping people become the kind of people we would like to have live in our own neighborhood.

The message is also clear that colleges need to practice truth in advertising and truth in outcomes and outcome assessment. Administrators need to make sure that the catalogues and all other information coming from the colleges are straightforward and that they do indeed practice full disclosure. They must look at the outcomes of their efforts critically and refrain from painting what they do and the results of such activities in rosy hues.

One of the points made by George Vaughan in the first chapter is worth returning to. One of the more serious ethical issues of our day in the world of community colleges is the lack of understanding of what community colleges are about and what they ought to be about. This would seem to be an untrue statement when we can observe the tidal wave of power that has swept through our nation via this unique institution. It is also true that virtually everyone can give a list of things colleges do to achieve their mission. We know that community colleges are open-door colleges, offering opportunity for local citizens to acquire the first two years of a program leading to a bachelor's degree. These institutions offer avenues that lead people to employment through technical and vocational programs. The colleges provide opportunity for special services to the community, access to cultural and avocational endeavors, and partnerships with business and industry as well. Developmental programs teaching basic skills would also be part of the litany in response to a question relating to mission.

The problem occurs when the questions Why are colleges doing this? and What is the compelling purpose of the institution? are asked. In the final analysis, can college leaders really sort and sift through everything and come up with an answer to these questions, and can they incisively ask questions that are provoking and can contribute to the desired end result?

The issue divides itself into two distinct parts. First, it has to do with understanding the people who have been touched by our colleges. How have these people become more whole? Second, it focuses on the offerings that help the colleges to reach their compelling purpose in the most effective way. More anecdotal than substantive evidence contributes to an understanding of how colleges can help to create more complete human beings and develop ways to know how well this is being done.

College leaders cannot take the easy way out and be flag-wavers for community colleges without getting answers to the questions of why colleges perform their missions and how effective colleges are in creating a better society. College leaders simply must move more dramatically to answer these questions. Otherwise, they can hardly cover themselves in a mantle of ethical behavior.

A recurring theme in the preceding chapters is that endless

discussions on ethics and ethical decision making should take place among the entire community college family. Every effort must be made to ensure that the environment for such discussions is one that affords great openness and encourages people to share to the fullest. The value of practicing the principles of "listening to understand" and "speaking to be understood" is a powerful point made in previous chapters.

Daniel Moriarty, in Chapter Three, speaks of the need to create codes of ethics. From my perspective, there is little question about the merit of this recommendation, for I believe that the creation of such codes is extremely valuable. We would be remiss, however, if we did not realize that the process is likely to be worth more than the actual code. The immersion and re-immersion of all concerned in the process of creating such codes is mandatory; otherwise, the code will lose power and the creators of the code will fail to capitalize on the great good that can come from such a process.

Another clear message from previous chapters is that the ethical tone for the institution is set by the president and the board. A related anecdote comes from Robert K. Greenleaf (n.d.): "It is reported that a king once asked Confucius what to do about thievery among his subjects. The answer was, 'If you, sir, were not covetous, they would not steal—even if you urged them to do it.' The idea is very old; if you want to reform something, begin with yourself—no matter who you are and how moral and correct a person you believe yourself to be" (p. 1).

The president truly is the key person in setting the tone on campus. The role of the board in setting the tone is also critically important. Daniel Moriarty in Chapter Three sums up the concept very well when he says that presidents who empower constituents, share leadership responsibilities, and insist on individual initiative and responsibility are executives who believe in human possibilities and the power of people to renew themselves and their societies. This empowerment can come from people at every level, not just the president or the board members. The ethical failure of a college is not an indictment of everyone at the college. Some people persevere even when top leadership fails. Some ethical heroics go without fanfare and do much good. Ethical leadership can be exercised from every position within the college.

## The Reflection of Community Values in the College

If we focus on our community colleges and the people who are a part of the college family, we will see them, in part, as reflections of the general values and mores of the communities they serve. This reflection is unquestionably a source of great strength to our institutions. It also is important to understand that the shadowy side of our communities abides in our colleges as well. If we were to study the human animal and take a page from the teachings of Carl Jung, we surely would recognize that shadowy side. Recognizing all the baggage brought into our institutions by close connections with communities should not diminish the pride college leaders feel in their grass-roots institutions that can quickly respond to the needs of people.

To varying degrees, each community college finds a multiplicity of views on ethics and patterns of behavior as part of its makeup. Quick reflection points up some of the reasons for this. Boards are elected or appointed by people who have special interests that are not always well motivated or fair. Boards tend to mirror the culture from which they come. Presidents have similar problems as they try to work closely with the community and find themselves either conforming to business as usual or having to make tough decisions that are sometimes not popular.

Some individuals see community colleges as having ethical dilemmas different from those of society in general. Often, however, while the dilemmas faced by campus leaders are very similar to dilemmas faced by society in general, the issues take on new dimensions because of the campus setting. Most professions and organizations tend to see more problems in ethics in other professions or organizations than in their own. Things are always worse somewhere else. We tend to practice intellectual celibacy when we see other people's lapses; that is, we criticize others for things we might do. For example, college leaders may be critical when people are hired or contracts awarded based upon friendship or upon political or personal financial considerations in city or state government but may excuse the same choices for community colleges. They fail to see the similarity between colleges that elevate enrollments through deceptive practices and those municipalities that pad certain figures in order to qualify for federal government programs.

To address the issue of community college ethics, college leaders must first be willing to attack some of the precedents, some of the mythology, some of the destructive baggage, and some of the traditional excuses for behavior that misdirect people's efforts as they seek to arrive at an ethical decision-making process. Attacking these areas not only can be helpful in the operations of community colleges but can also have great impact on the nation as a whole through community college leadership.

Here again I turn to the work of Michael Josephson. Obviously, one's values and ideas about ethics are shaped by a lifetime of living, reading, and observing. Still, a great deal of credit goes to Josephson for bringing together an advanced decision-making process and for adding his personal stamp to this effort.

Josephson (1990) indicates some common attitudes about ethics that are important for us to know and accept. These include such concepts as the following:

1. The vast majority of people in every walk of life accept the notion that it is important to be ethical.
2. Most people are concerned about the failure of others, individually and as members of influential professions, to live up to high ethical standards.
3. There is a general consensus on a core group of values that people associate with being ethical.
4. Most people believe that their profession as a whole is more ethical and responsible than other professions.
5. Most people believe that they are more ethical than others in society in general and in their profession.
6. To maintain the belief that they are ethical, people tend to elevate their professional goals to moral imperatives.

It is important to see these six common attitudes as describing conditions in our society and therefore in the community college family in this nation. Recognition of these attitudes logically dictates that some myths that seem to be generally accepted in our society need to be identified and debunked.

## The Mythology of Ethics

A number of myths continue to influence how decisions are made. These myths must not be used as an excuse for unethical behavior. Among the most prominent myths are the following:

### Myth One: If It Is Legal, It Is Ethical

On every hand in today's society, we see people take refuge in legalities. Such an approach has engendered great mistrust and suspicion. In the biography of William Casey by Joseph E. Persico, Robert Inman is quoted as saying, "Bill Casey was a free-lance buccaneer. If I had to sum him up in one sentence, I'd put it this way. If it's not specifically prohibited by law, then it's okay. Do it" (Persico, 1990, p. 298). Yet most people would agree that there is something more important than just being legal. There is a condition of rightness or wrongness. We know it is quite possible to behave within the letter of the law and still be unethical. One could be a true scalawag, the kind of person that most people would not want for a neighbor, and still be behaving legally but certainly not ethically.

Over and over, our culture has been influenced by individuals, particularly leaders in Congress and the executive branch and leading business executives, who have taken refuge in the law and claimed that this legality cleansed them of all wrongdoing. It is understandable that people trying to avoid prison terms for their actions will claim anything that will keep them from such a fate. However, if we continue to equate being legal with being ethical, we are obviously in a great deal of trouble.

This attitude, unfortunately, is common in community colleges as well. Most readers will know of situations in which this attitude is displayed by college presidents and trustees. For example, in at least one state, the attorney general said that it was acceptable for the spouse of a board member to be employed in a high-level administrative position at the college as long as the board member abstained from voting on the matter of employment. The decision to employ the woman, though legal, gave no consideration to the potential ethical problems. This situation raises several ethical questions. What burden does the situation place on the president in evaluating the woman? What pressure does the vote place upon the abstaining member's fellow board members in votes concerning the spouse? What kind of atmosphere does the presence of the woman create in the institution?

## Myth Two: If You Have a Right to Do It, It Is the Right Thing to Do

This myth is a spin-off of myth one in many ways. One example of how this myth manifests itself is a situation in which a trustee in a closed meeting of the board dealing with a personnel matter or a collective bargaining issue might think, Because I have my First Amendment rights and I have freedom of speech, it is perfectly all right for me to disclose everything that was discussed in this meeting. This disclosure is not right because it destroys trust. And it destroys other basic principles that are among the list of common values, even though it is perfectly legal and even though the person has a right to do it.

To realize that the right thing to do means curtailing activities or words that one has a right to do or to say is most helpful in destroying this myth. As trustees more deeply understand what it means to support a president and move always to help create an environment that enhances the president's ability to function, doing the right thing takes on a special dimension for them. To live by the rule of no surprises is very important for trustees and presidents. This rule, when properly understood, helps trustees and presidents realize that there is an active side to this issue as well as a passive one. Trustees and presidents must go out of their way not only to not surprise each other but also to communicate in such a way with each other as to help the institution look good and be good. The board member who lets the president know ahead of the board meeting what concerns he or she has is following the rule of no surprises. This rule is important in creating an environment for a high level of ethical decision making.

*Myth Three: If People Are Not Ethical by the Time They Are
Adults, It Is Too Late for Them to Change*

This myth is frequently cited as a reason not to attempt to change.
Certainly, changing the patterns of people with ingrained habits
and wrong values is far more difficult than training a young person.
Community colleges have been in the forefront of dealing with
society's problems and need not run from the issue of taking people
from where they are and moving them progressively forward as far
as it is possible to do so.

Ethical behavior is not simply a matter of character. It truly
is a matter of decision making. As Josephson (1990) has stated,
"Ethics are advanced one decision at a time. The issue is not all or
nothing (always being ethical); it is a question of being more ethical
more often" (p. 2). This premise would tend to bring some relax-
ation to our discussions of ethics and some clear hope for real progress through an ethical decision-making process. Probably none of
us will always be ethical, but all of us can be more ethical more
often.

*Myth Four: If You Have a Code of Ethics, Things Will Be
Dramatically Improved*

Some of the most horrendous things have occurred in institutions
that have a code of ethics. My observations cause me to believe that
the process of creating a code of ethics is worth more than the code
itself. This would seem to lead to the conclusion that community
colleges need to repeatedly hold sessions on ethical issues.

An awareness and understanding of the four myths is essential in instituting any ethical decision-making process. The same is
true for some special baggage we carry that weighs all too heavily
on us.

### The White Lie Baggage

The white lie creates an ethical insensitivity that contributes to the
problems just discussed. The white lie is often considered to be an
act of kindness, something that would help protect people. Diplo-

macy can be good, but if confused with the white lie, it loses its quality. Sometimes we try to make people feel better by lying. For example, we may say, "Gee, that was a good presentation" when we know that it was not.

Letters of recommendation in community colleges illustrate this point. Almost everyone acknowledges that letters of recommendation are not worth much. Sometimes the language in these letters is so obvious that we know that the truth is not being disclosed. College personnel who are concerned about ethical decision making need to address this issue and consider what really should take place.

We think that we protect our self-interest by telling white lies. We all recognize the scene in which the secretary answers the phone and asks the boss, "Are you in?" and the boss responds, "No, tell him I'm out." These kinds of lies generally indicate an unaccountability for ourselves and can easily shift problems or blame in a way that injures another person.

Sissela Bok in her book *Lying* (1978) has pointed out that deceit has a coercible quality about it that does not allow people to be able to act as they might otherwise. Bok (pp. 19–20) states:

> To the extent that knowledge gives power, lies affect the distribution of power; they add to that of the liar and diminish that of the deceived, altering his choices at different levels. Everyone depends on deception to get out of the scrape, to save face, to avoid hurting the feelings of others. Some use it more consciously to manipulate and gain ascendancy, yet all are intimately aware of the threat lies can pose, the suffering they can bring. Why are such radically different evaluations given to the effects of deception depending on whether the point of view is that of the liar or the one lied to?

There is little question that those who discover that they have been lied to, even through a white lie, become less trusting. Their attitudes and subsequent behavior are affected by knowing that they have been the recipient of a lie. If the question is posed, Does another person have the right to lie to me for my own good? not many people would say yes. Quoting again from Bok (1978): "They see that they were manipulated, that the deceit made them unable to make choices for themselves, according to the most adequate information available, unable to act as they would have wanted to act had they known all along. Of course, we know that many lies are trivial. Inasmuch as we have no way to judge which lies are the trivial ones, and since we have no confidence that liars will restrict themselves to just such trivial lies, the perspective of the deceived leads us to be wary of all deception" (pp. 20–21.).

Some examples of telling white lies that have an effect on community college operations follow. These white lies are frequently understood for what they are—lies. They undermine people's trust in the college and make the institutional climate less healthy. The trustee or president using a white lie is a role model for others in the institution to do the same.

- "I tried to get back to you while you were out." In fact, the speaker did not return the call at all.
- "I had some people mention to me that . . ." The speaker is using this phrase to indicate public opinion for something that is really only the speaker's opinion.
- "Well, I would like to visit longer, but I have someone waiting for me." The speaker really just wants to get off the phone.
- "We would like to accommodate your group, but the auditorium is scheduled for that week." The speaker does not want to book another country and western performance.
- "Dear _____, I just wanted to let you know how much all of us appreciated . . ." The writer has not even checked with anyone else.
- "We mailed that out just this morning." The speaker forgot to mail the material.
- "Sure, I remember you. I just cannot place where we met." The speaker does not recognize this person.
- "Wow, that is the first time I have heard of that." The speaker has known for weeks, but hoped no one would find out.
- "I'll have to check the files and get back to you." The speaker really just wants time to think up an excuse.

- "I would like to do this for you, but I have already turned down a number of people and I can't make an exception." The speaker really does not want to accommodate the request.

## The Competition Baggage

Given the culture of our society, we make an almost instinctive assumption that there is always and forever a justifiable right to win—to retain a job, to get legislation passed, to acquire the prestige or power we deserve or think we deserve—to reach whatever goals of winning or being first we may have. It is difficult for ambitious people who are success oriented to see that in a greater scheme of things there is not really a necessity or a justification to win.

All too often we look at the pursuit of excellence, one of our basic ethical principles, as a means to justify our self-interest. For instance, getting more state financial support for a community college in order to do good things has its down side. The competition among institutions to see which one can gain the most full-time equivalent students has led to shady practices in course offerings, student recruiting, and enrollment reporting. Some states that rely solely on an enrollment-driven formula for funding are accomplices in unethical behavior. The desire to win has resulted in a number of potentially corrupting endeavors. Some of these are to win a national athletic championship, to get recognition for having placed the most presidents at other institutions, and to get recognition for the best program in the country in some field.

Our quest for excellence frequently is a quest to beat someone, to get ahead, to be first—never mind the price, never mind how we do it. We fail to address the more important questions—What do I really need to do that is sound and ethical? What can I do to help others get what they need through appropriate behavior? What is the true meaning of excellence?

The issue of competition is an interesting one because it is part and parcel of our nation's culture and therefore is part of the culture of the community college. For all of the good that has come from athletic competition, for instance, we can easily see the devastating problems that result from the pressure to win and to be number one. It is quite evident that the environment that has been created seems to put such a value on winning and being number one that great numbers of people have engaged in unethical behavior and have created unfair situations for a great majority of our people. This way of life is part of our legacy to future generations.

In some community colleges, an objective observer might easily conclude that athletics was the most important ingredient of the institution and that winning a national championship was the most important goal. This quest can become consuming to the degree that it corrupts the entire institution and the lives of many young people.

Some illumination of the issue of competition comes to us through Eastern religion. The Tao reveals some interesting things about power and competition. Schuang Tsu's poem "The Need to Win" brings home something that strikes a chord of recognition in most of us. The poem does not oppose winning. It is a paradox. It simply says that the only way to victory is to forget victory. For example, a community college should strive to be as good as it can be rather than to beat another institution. The college may not get national or even regional recognition, but the college's goal is powerful and augers well for all those whose lives are touched by the college.

Doing our best is healthy. Trying to be the best has great appeal, but it is fraught with peril. Ethical misbehavior is not as likely to happen in an environment where doing one's best is emphasized rather than beating others. Those who are thoughtful about leadership know that the desire for success and the fear of failure sometimes pervert action and can even lead to wrongdoing. Being caught up in winning and losing is a false framework in which to operate, and we can become possessed by unhealthy power.

A dramatic example of the power of doing one's best rather than being caught up in the negative side of competition comes from the work of community college presidents who have served as interim presidents. These interim presidents are amazing in that they have come to the presidency relaxed, focused, and wanting the best. They are trying to do their best, trying to give their best. They take time to talk and listen to people, to connect with people, and to make the right kind of assessments. They are not ruffled, tense, or pressured. They feel at ease. They feel that they can make accurate decisions and they do generally make accurate decisions. The people in the institution deeply appreciate the leadership they display. There is a powerful lesson here in what it means to do one's best and not feel the tension that goes with trying to be the best. Doing one's best rather than being driven to be number one creates a much improved climate for ethical decision making.

Our ethical responsibility is increased by trying to do our best because all of our decisions must take into account other people and how they are affected. The exercise of considering all of the stakeholders affected by any decision gives the golden rule a prominent place in our thinking. A list of ethical values and principles is also essential. If community college administrators consider their decisions with the understanding that these principles always take precedence over nonethical possibilities, they can make major improvements in the operations of community colleges.

## Conclusion

Ethical decision making becomes more difficult when we have to decide between two conflicting ethical principles. This difficult situation demands that we have finely tuned sensitivities that cannot come about easily in the absence of a commitment to being more ethical more of the time.

The issue of fairness is raised when student needs come into conflict with faculty needs. These situations are frequently colored by the collective bargaining process. They are complicated further by the emotions engendered through long-standing friendships. But any process that causes decision makers to consider all of the stakeholders and to consider several possible ethical alternatives will bear fruit.

No amount of lecturing, sermonizing, or commiserating over bad behavior will change the behavior. We simply will continue to wallow in the mud of the past. Business as usual will not be sufficient. One of the sad results of business as usual is that it diminishes the beauty of what the community college is all about in its commitment to serve others. Greenleaf's statement as to what institutions ought to be about is appropriate. He says that what should happen to people because of having been touched by our community colleges is simply this: the colleges leave us "wiser, healthier, freer, more autonomous, more able to serve others, and . . . the least privileged in our society are better off" (1991, p. 36).

The questions to be asked following that statement include Can this goal be met as effectively in an environment that is not highly ethical? and Can this goal be met in the absence of a concerted effort to focus on the issue of ethics? The quality of our future depends on the answers. One simple but powerful tool is the use of the previously suggested icon. The vision of the icon trust, when fully understood, can serve as a beacon for an enlightened future, that bodes well for improved behavior and wiser decisions on our campuses.

The answer to ethical problems seems always to lie in educational processes. Sensitivity and awareness can be heightened through these processes, and we must commit to whatever it takes to make people aware of the consequences of unethical actions. There is no panacea, but the importance of making ethical decisions the foundation for each community college demands action. Institutions that involve themselves in consensus making and work to empower people rather than to strengthen hierarchical structure are much more apt to create an environment conducive to ethical behavior than are others. Shared governance on campus is one safeguard against unethical behavior.

This book has a number of golden nuggets for the reader. It is diverse and rich in its ability to stimulate the open-minded reader. The challenge for community college leaders is simply to get more serious about cause and effect in the arena of ethical behavior. Such seriousness will force every community college to engage in discussions that will result in a higher sensitivity to ethical issues and a way to make decisions that will raise our ethical batting average.

The icon of trust can become a powerful reminder to all of us if we take time to make it more fully illuminated and meaningful. In the final analysis all the authors of this book speak to issues that, if considered and solved, build trust. Who among us could have a higher calling?

## References

Bok, S. *Lying.* New York: Pantheon, 1978.

Greenleaf, R. K. "The Servant as Leader." Indianapolis, Ind. R. K. Greenleaf Center, 1991.

Greenleaf, R. K. "A Lifeline of Ideas." Unpublished paper, Andover-Newton Seminary Archives, Newton, Mass., n.d.

Josephson, M. "The Josephson Institute Training Program for Ethics Educators." Unpublished paper, Josephson Institute, 1990.

Persico, J. E. *Casey.* New York: Viking Penguin, 1990.

Tyler, G. "Education and the New Millenium." *AGB Reports,* July–Aug. 1991, 33–35.

# Index

## A

Academic freedom: and classroom issues, 87; and linkages, 139–140; and trustees, 165
Academic Skills Program, 44
Accountability: and code of ethics, 66; as value, 156–157, 162
Administration, ethical issues of, 90–92, 190–207
Adorno, T. W., 84, 93
Advertising: and affirmative action, 180–181, 182; inflated, 34–35; truth in, 193
Affirmative action: ethical issues of, 90–92, 115–117; ethical practice and, 179–182
Affirmative opportunity, and search process, 180, 181–182
Alger, H., 48
American Association of Community and Junior Colleges (AACJC), 36, 66, 69, 144; Educational Business Activities Policy

Statement of, 133; Keeping America Working project of, 128; Presidents Academy of, 10, 99, 137; Putting America Back to Work project of, 128
American Association of State Colleges and Universities, 10, 99
American Association of University Professors, 87, 99
American College Testing Program, 44
American Council on Education, 12, 100, 128, 144, 181–182, 188
Aristotle, 53
Ashby, E., 9, 11, 27, 28
Aslanian, C. B., 125, 129, 145
Association of California Community College Administrators, 10
Associations: and codes of ethics, 10, 66, 69, 87; ethics statements from, 99; reportage from, 35–36; and teaching of ethics, 77
Authoritarianism, and faculty ethics, 84

**209**

sions of, 24–25, 56, 67–69, 100–
103, 108–109, 149, 193, 195;
disruptions from, 149; and
higher education, 8–13, 30–31,
97–123; of ignoring, 30–50; and
institutional culture, 19–22; in
instructional programs, 73–96,
105–106, 113–115; and leadership, 1–70; and legality, 198–199;
lessons on, 192–195; misconceptions about, 147–150; of moral
leadership, 53–55; myths on,
198–200; policies and practices
for, 71–168; and rights, 199; and
rule of reason, 6–8; in selection
process, 171–174; and standards
of leadership, 169–207; and
white lies, 200–203
Evaluation, ethical practice for,
172, 184–188
Excellence, as value, 156

**F**

Faculty: academic scruples for, 97–
123; authoritarianism and sexual harassment by, 84–87; and
business and community linkages, 141–142; demographic features of, 80; ethical issues for,
79–87; hiring practices for, 90–
92, 93; and presidential selection, 176; professionalism of,
82–83, 142–143; responsibilities
of, 62; as role models, 80–82, 89,
91, 101
Fairness, as value, 151–152
Fass, R. A., 90, 94
Federal Trade Commission, 35, 36
Feldman, M. J., 125, 132, 137, 144
Fidelity, as value, 153–154
Finance: and business and community linkages, 138–141; ethical
issues in, 107–108, 120–121
Fisk, E. C., 33, 50
Florida: economic restraints in, 4;
outcome measures in, 42, 44
Frankel, M. S., 66, 70
Frenkel-Brunswik, E., 84, 93

Freud, S., 84
Friedan, B., 54
Friedman, J., 52

**G**

Gandhi, M., 54
Gardner, J. W., 53–54, 55, 61, 70,
98, 123
General education, and linkages,
137–138
Germany, National Socialist party
in, 165
Gifts, from businesses, 138–139
Gordon, E. W., 31–32, 49
Gottleber, T. T., 75–76, 94
Governing boards. *See* Trustees
Grant, U. S., 78
Greenfield, R., 14
Greenleaf, R. K., 195, 205–206, 207
Griffin, W. A., Jr., 90, 94

**H**

Hagerstown Junior College, ethics
colloquium of, 79
Hamilton, J., 127, 144
Hankin, J. N., 97
Harding, W. G., 78
Harvard University: Graduate
School of Education at, 9; Institute for Educational Management at, 9
Hawaii, University of, harassment
policies of, 87
Hays, G., 187, 189
Hazard Community College, Business and Industry Technical Assistance Center of, 141–142
Hazard-Perry Chamber of Commerce, 141
Higher education: academic scruples in, 97–123; background on,
97–98; conclusion on, 121–122;
and ethics, 8–13, 30–31; ethics
audit for, 108–109; moral dilemmas in, 98–108, 109–121. *See also*
Community colleges
Hill, A., 84

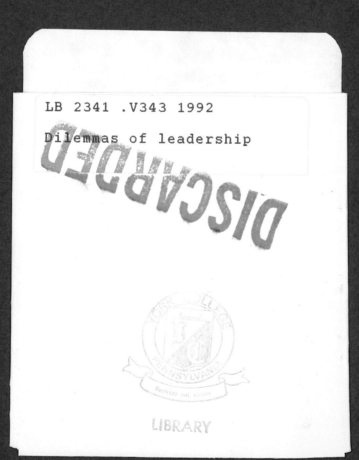